Mugwumps

Mugwumps

PUBLIC MORALISTS
OF THE GILDED AGE

David M. Tucker

University of Missouri Press

Columbia and London

Copyright © 1998 by
The Curators of the University of Missouri
University of Missouri Press, Columbia, Missouri 65201
Printed and bound in the United States of America
All rights reserved
5 4 3 2 1   02 01 00 99 98

Library of Congress Cataloging-in-Publication Data

Tucker, David M., 1937–
   Mugwumps : public moralists of the gilded age / David M. Tucker.
     p.   cm.
   Includes bibliographical references (p.   ) and index.
   ISBN 0-8262-1187-9 (alk. paper)
   1. Social reformers—United States—History.   2. Ethicists—United
States—History.   3. Social justice.   I. Title.
HN57.T77   1998
303.48'4'0973—dc21   98-20718
                                                            CIP

♾™ This paper meets the requirements of the
American National Standard for Permanence of Paper
for Printed Library Materials, Z39.48, 1984.

Text design: Elizabeth K. Young
Jacket design: Susan Ferber
Typesetter: BookComp, Inc.
Printer and binder: Thomson-Shore, Inc.
Typefaces: Minion and Minion Condensed

   Permission to quote from the Adams Family Papers has been granted by
The Adams Manuscript Trust, Massachusetts Historical Society, Boston.
   Permission has also been granted to quote from *Letters of Henry Adams,*
edited by J. C. Levenson, E. Samuels, C. Vandersee, and V. H. Winner,
Copyright 1982, 1984 by the Massachusetts Historical Society, Reprinted
by permission of Harvard University Press.

Contents

Preface

Mugwumps were nineteenth-century reformers concerned with public virtue—doing the right thing in American life and government. They were the college educated who lived the lessons of their moral philosophy, that blend of Christian values, republican virtue, and classical liberalism that distinguished Mugwump ethics. Abolitionists and Republican party moralists before the Civil War, they continued to act out their public values in the Gilded Age, lecturing party leaders who shifted from moral principle to office-holding partisanship, private-interest politics, and territorial imperialism.

The Mugwump mix of values and politics has been ridiculed by the last generation of scholars, who regarded ethical concerns as irrelevant for politics. The conventional academic wisdom of the twentieth century has been that morality has little to do with the practice of politics and that any significant change must be pursued within a major party. The independents have even been accused of ruining popular partisan politics by turning campaigns into educational forums that lowered voter turnout.

The trouble with influential studies of Mugwumpery from the 1950s and 1960s is that they took a very cynical reading of Mugwump words and actions. The generation of Richard Hofstadter, *The Age of Reform* (1955), Ari Hoogenboom, *Outlawing the Spoils* (1961), and John Sproat, *"The Best Men"* (1968) raised their eyebrows at every mention of morality and searched elsewhere for convincing motivation. Defenders of the Democratic New Deal assumed any reformer who trusted the capitalist market more than government intervention was hopelessly outdated and unworthy of the term "liberal." Mugwumps were really conservatives, it was said, motivated by bitterness against the successful of their day. The hard-boiled realists of the Hofstadter generation refused to take seriously

Mugwump talk of free markets, free soil, free labor, free speech, and free trade. Mugwumps were dismissed as narrow-minded, impractical conservatives suffering from declining status and irrational resentments.

And yet, if you consider that these public moralists won all five of their major reforms—two in their lifetime (abolition of slavery and civil service reform), and three in the next century (stripping Congress of its money-printing power, depriving manufacturers of control over tariff policy, and ending American imperialism), Mugwumps do seem relevant. To exert influence on important problems in a democracy is surely enough for applause. Without Mugwumps we could take less pride in our past.

Understanding Mugwumps begins with a book students memorized in the decades before the Civil War. Francis Wayland's *The Elements of Moral Science* (1835) promoted a Christian ethics beginning with love of God, keeping the Sabbath, and including chastity, veracity, and benevolence. *Moral Science* taught religion as morality, repressing the base interests of self and promoting the welfare of others, the general welfare, and the republic. Wayland's moral philosophy reflected the republican faith in civic virtue, which rejected citizen use of government to enhance self- or class interest. The individual must serve God and community in political life rather than self. Wayland specifically insisted that individuals commit to principles and not to political parties. Students who lived their moral philosophy lessons went on to become Mugwumps; others went on to become opportunists in pursuing self-interest. Perhaps no opportunist sunk so low as Benjamin F. Butler, who memorized Wayland's *Moral Science* and then broke all the rules. A creature of self-interest, Butler refused to become a Republican or an abolitionist before the Civil War, and then opportunistically turned into a radical Republican spoilsman who ridiculed civil service reform, free trade, and hard money. Butler characterized the opposite of a Mugwump.

Mugwumps retained a passionate grip on the ethics of *Moral Science*, but as intellectuals they suffered loss of faith in the theology of Wayland. After Darwin published *The Origin of Species* (1859), they rejected the existence of God but continued to advocate morality, science, and education as the path to progress. Dropping traditional religion led no Mugwumps to abandon traditional ethics; these Victorians continued their ethical code of moral character and altruism. They were obsessed with avoiding selfishness. These were men of character who sought to overcome selfish appetites, focusing instead on the welfare of others. They had been educated to be public moralists.

While the origins of Mugwump thought were clearly in antebellum moral education, the best existing study of the reformers begins a generation later, in 1884, the year these independents helped swing the presidential election to the Democrat candidate Grover Cleveland. Gerald W. McFarland's *Mugwumps, Morals, and Politics* (1975) profiles the campaign of 1884, provides an excellent socioeconomic profile of the reformers, and traces their work into the twentieth century, but his book begins in the middle of the Mugwump story.

An earlier study, John G. Sproat's *"The Best Men"* (1968), included the independent Republican reform efforts of the 1870s but neglected the antebellum Mugwump origins. The chief weakness of *"The Best Men,"* however, reflected a 1960s disdain for morality, elites, and leadership. Sproat's distaste for these reformers created a caricature of them as self-righteous, antidemocratic, insensitive prigs. To be sure some of these disagreeable qualities did exist, but any balanced portrait of Mugwumps must include their positive role in persuading politicians to eliminate slavery from America, to oppose special interests, and to promote public morality. Politicians always needed encouragement to do the right thing, and even if the advice was rarely followed, critics were not necessarily failures. Mugwumps were given their reputation for failure by later cheerleaders for the welfare state. While reformers enjoyed a great reputation in their own time, in the next century, after the Great Depression of the 1930s turned educated opinion to Keynesian economics, nineteenth-century liberals who feared government as the enemy of freedom and progress were recast as selfish, wrongheaded agents for the middle class.

Mugwumps can best be understood as public moralists. They never saw themselves as agents for an economic class. Admission to their world was gained by promoting public and not private interests. Their training in moral philosophy compelled them to unite their personal virtue with the lessons from social science to promote the general welfare. Their sense of public morality, their obsession with avoiding self-interest, was so keen that benevolence and altruism were their substitutes for religion. Personal virtue was a central concern for Mugwumps; they felt good about themselves when they were benevolent. They participated in politics and advocated free-market economics not to advance any self-interest but to promote the public welfare and to perform their altruistic duty. The effects of their economic liberalism may not always have been so altruistic as they believed, but any society is fortunate to have public moralists who put the common good above the interest of their class. And Mugwump efforts merit a sympathetic retelling from a study of ten who were the major voices of Mugwumpery. Henry Adams, Charles Francis Adams Jr., Edward Atkinson, E. L. Godkin, Charles Eliot Norton, Carl Schurz, Moorfield Storey, William Graham Sumner, David A. Wells, and Horace White thus shape this book.

Mugwumps

1

Moral Virtue from College

The nineteenth-century American college lived to moralize, to promote the moral character prescribed by evangelical Protestant religion. Antebellum college presidents were Christian ministers for whom piety and strength of character were central college purposes. The president of Brown expressed that goal plainly in 1842, saying: "The most important end to be secured in the education of the young is moral character. Without this, brilliancy of intellect will only plunge its possessor more deeply in temporal disgrace and eternal misery."[1] The traditional college never intended to turn out secular scientists or humanists but men who believed that moral virtue should govern private and public life.

The moral indoctrination of college students could be observed in required chapel and especially in Moral Philosophy—the senior ethics course that sought to prepare graduates for Christian leadership. This product of Enlightenment and evangelical thought promoted an intellectually respectable Christian ethics and public philosophy. This course taught virtue—doing the right thing on public and private issues—to prepare graduates to become the moral elite of community and nation.[2]

This required course usually assigned one text—*The Elements of Moral Science* (1835)—written by a Baptist minister and college president. President Francis Wayland was a New Yorker, born in 1796, the son of strict English immigrant parents who had shifted from business to Baptist

1. Francis Wayland, *Thoughts on the Present Collegiate System in the United States,* 115; Laurence R. Veysey, *The Emergence of the American University,* 21–28; D. H. Meyer, *The Instructed Conscience: The Shaping of the American National Ethic,* 114–15.
2. George P. Schmidt, *The Old Time College President,* 108–16; Wilson Smith, *Professors and Public Ethics: Studies of Northern Moral Philosophers before the Civil War,* 9; Meyer, *Instructed Conscience,* 18, 63; Daniel Walker Howe, *The Unitarian Conscience: Harvard Moral Philosophy, 1805–1861,* 1–4.

preaching. The son rejected the rigid Calvinism of the father and planned to become a medical doctor rather than a minister. On graduating from Union College, he studied medicine and began to practice as a physician, when a more permissive Baptist persuaded him that he might become a minister even though he had enjoyed no striking conversion experience. Wayland abandoned medicine for a ministry of modified Calvinism in which people were considered rational moral beings. His college degree and theology study at the Andover Theological School marked him an educated minister in an unlettered denomination. Academic credentials brought Wayland to the attention of a struggling First Baptist Boston, which was seeking a minister who would not embarrass them before Harvard Unitarians. First Baptist hired the tall, thin, reserved Wayland even though he lacked a popular preaching style and read his sermons from written manuscripts. Scholarly sermons made little impact on the congregation, but when the first was printed in 1825, Wayland won recognition across the Protestant community. Two years later the thirty-one-year-old Wayland was unanimously selected to become president of Brown, the Baptist college in Rhode Island.[3]

Wayland thrived as college president, removing beer from the student center, raising the moral tone of the school, and delivering chapel talks and moral philosophy lectures that became the standard text in American colleges. When he began teaching, the common moral philosophy text had been the more permissive William Paley, *Moral and Political Philosophy* (1785). To be sure, Paley had been a British minister with a Christian view of morality, but American evangelicals were unhappy with his utilitarianism. When Paley asked where we should turn for guidance, when neither law nor Scriptures provide direction, his answer had been that we, ourselves, promote the general happiness. Paley reasoned that God wanted our happiness, and therefore we were doing his will when we promoted the general happiness. Yet pleasure and joy sounded too secular or immoral for Wayland and other evangelicals, who preferred a dour Scottish conscience as the moral guide for young men.[4]

President Wayland sought to shift ethics away from utilitarianism and back to the individual conscience and the supernatural sanction. The God who created the world and its moral laws, Wayland said, had also given

3. Francis Wayland Jr. and H. L. Wayland, *A Memoir of the Life and Labors of Francis Wayland*, 12–203; James O. Murray, *Francis Wayland*, 45; Joseph L. Blau, *Men and Movements in American Philosophy*, 82–88.

4. Smith, *Professors and Public Ethics*, 38, 41, 187–88; Murray, *Francis Wayland*, 200–201.

us a conscience or moral sense to tell us what to do. Just as God's natural law of gravity kept the planets in orbit, so did God's moral code manage the fate of individuals and nations. Our conscience intuitively knew the law of God and could govern our appetites, passions, reason, and will. Of course, President Wayland admitted the conscience could sometimes make mistakes and should be properly educated and trained. The conscience worked like a muscle, which can be strengthened by use and impaired by disuse. Every time we gain a victory over our lower propensities, acquire self-control, our conscience and our Christian character grow in strength and virtue.[5]

Evangelical Protestants applauded Wayland's reinstatement of the supernatural sanction for morality and his packaging of the message in scientific language. His *Moral Science* presented the moral law as absolute, just like the laws of physics, math, and chemistry. The text claimed to approximate the rigor of the physical sciences in discovering the rules for human behavior. God created a world of predictable consequences for physical and moral actions, it was said. The consequences of a wrong decision were inevitable; every violation of the moral law of the Creator would be punished. This text was destined for popularity because it briefly introduced the theory of moral law and the existence of a conscience, and then the remaining two-thirds of the book provided concrete examples of practical ethics based on Bible teachings. *Moral Science* quickly replaced Paley, eventually selling a hundred thousand copies and becoming the most widely read American text.[6]

Wayland taught that Christian moral virtue determined the success of individuals and nations. If Americans lacked the virtues of honesty, chastity, benevolence, justice, and piety, then neither the Constitution nor the Supreme Court could save the United States government. "If we possess that required amount of virtue," Wayland said, "the government will stand; if not, it will fall." In a republic, with control in the hands of voters, citizens were morally obligated to educate their children both intellectually and morally, and to vote for political candidates according to conscience and not according to party. Any politician who used power for the benefit of section or party was "false to his duty, to his country, and to his God."[7] No college student could have graduated without hearing that independence from political party was a moral virtue.

5. Francis Wayland, *The Elements of Moral Science*, 17–18, 42–75.
6. Ibid., 19, xiii.
7. Ibid., 328, 330.

Virtue always seemed an absolute, never a matter of opinion, in the study of moral science, which Wayland defined as the systematic arrangement of laws established by God. Those laws were said to be found in the Bible, which provided the foundation for both the science of moral philosophy and political economy, a related subject for which Wayland also published a text, *Elements of Political Economy* (1837).

Political economy and moral philosophy studied separate subject matter, but Wayland considered both to be scientific studies of God's laws. His book described the economic world as running according to laws established by God. This beneficial system had been explained by Adam Smith two generations before in *Wealth of Nations* (1776). Wayland never adopted Smith's phrase "invisible hand," but he certainly continued his understanding that God's laws regulated the pursuit of wealth for the mutual benefit of all. God had programmed people to work, Wayland said; if they wanted to eat, they had to work. And God had implanted desires for a variety of goods that required people to exchange goods and labor with others. Market behavior seemed evidence of God's plan for a peaceful world. Markets were not battles but mutually beneficial exchanges. While war destroyed, peaceful markets multiplied goods and services. God's law of mutual dependence required people to live in peace and conduct themselves upon principles of benevolence. Just as the self-interest of a butcher required him to treat his customer well, so should a nation treat other nations according to the principles of benevolence, the golden rule. Merchants or nations who impoverished customers would soon have none to trade with. People helped themselves by helping others. God's law of supply and demand was checked by his law of benevolence. These laws made free-market capitalists live by the golden rule rather than the jungle rule of tooth, claw, and force.[8]

Laws of the market seemed designed to promote moral behavior. Wayland thought divine law had legislated that "no man can grow rich without industry and frugality." Since moral virtue led to material wealth, he reasoned, the best means of promoting either economic growth or a republican government was by circulating the Scriptures and preaching the gospel. The Bible promoted industry, frugality, virtue, and intelligence, making peoples rich and governments just. God was surely an advocate of the work ethic, republican government, and Adam Smith liberalism. In the market, people helped themselves by helping others. If individuals were

8. Francis Wayland, *The Elements of Political Economy*, 15, 121, 163, 175.

left free and virtuous, and governments legislated no special privileges, such as protective tariffs, then Wayland was certain that wealth, love of right, and the golden rule would follow.[9]

Human slavery offended Wayland as the worst denial of individual liberty and greatest violation of God's laws of political economy and moral philosophy. God's moral precepts in the New Testament clearly opposed slavery, according to President Wayland, who cited key Biblical golden-rule precepts: "Thou shalt love thy neighbor as thyself, and all things whatsoever ye would that men should do unto you, do ye even so unto them," declaring them to be absolutely subversive of slavery, a system that was disastrous to the morals of all. Slavery cultivated vices in the master—pride, anger, cruelty, selfishness, and licentiousness—while fostering in the slave lying, deceit, hypocrisy, dishonesty, and a willingness to yield to the appetites of the master. Every Christian master had the duty of immediate emancipation before God himself acted against slavery. "The Judge of the whole earth will do justice," Wayland promised. "He hears the cry of the oppressed and He will, in the end, terribly vindicate right."[10]

Abolition of slavery and independence from political parties were positions of conscience that students of moral philosophy learned in the North after 1835. They were taught that if all virtuous men withdrew from the tyranny of political party and united instead on the moral principle of personal liberty, reformed parties and the reformed nation would soon reflect their moral character. But while *Moral Science* encouraged antislavery sentiment, Wayland would be labeled a conservative by William Lloyd Garrison, who condemned him as "that selfish and cowardly teacher of morality, President Wayland."[11] The trouble between the two began in 1831 when Wayland asked Garrison to send no more copies of *The Liberator,* which he found unwise and unchristian in tactics. By calling for immediate emancipation, it seemed to Wayland, Garrison rejected cool discussion with masters and excited rebellion in slaves. War and bloodshed were not the Christian way for Wayland or Garrison; they were both for nonviolence. The difference was only one of style. Of course a college president would talk more of Christian benevolence, forgiveness and good will to all; rather than menacing masters, a professor

9. Ibid., 137–38.
10. Wayland, *Elements of Moral Science,* 188–98.
11. Murray, *Francis Wayland,* 276–77, 203–4; Louis Ruchames, ed., *The Letters of William Lloyd Garrison,* (Cambridge: Harvard University Press, 1971), 3:263.

would prepare blacks for freedom and persuade masters of the error of slavery.[12]

But students of Wayland did slip from his Christian nonviolence, resorting to guns in defense of individual liberty. One of those was Horace White, a New Hampshire–born journalist who grew up on the Wisconsin frontier. In the local Beloit College he studied Wayland's text for his senior year (1852–1853) course in the moral philosophy taught by his Yale-educated college president. White committed to abolitionism and chose a career in journalism to further the crusade against slavery. As a Chicago reporter, White declared Abraham Lincoln's first speech against the expansion of slavery "the greatest ever listened to in the state of Illinois. . . ." Moving beyond reporting to direct involvement, White participated in the abolitionist war in Kansas Territory, serving as assistant secretary of the New England Emigrant Aid Company, escorting Sharps rifles to arm John Brown's army.[13]

The violent road to human freedom departed from Wayland's teachings, but even the teacher took the same journey. For two decades Wayland taught gradual moral suasion and peaceful emancipation. He hated slavery but refused to condemn slaveholders as sinners because, he thought, God had taken a moderate approach in the Bible, never directly prohibiting slavery but declaring moral precepts that, when understood properly, would end the practice of enslaving others. Wayland understood the biblical strategy of indirectly attacking slavery to be the best stealth-approach to convert slaveholders. Direct denunciation would turn masters from Christianity, while gradual moral suasion promised to lead to peaceful emancipation. He led the fight in 1845 to prevent abolitionists from expelling slaveholders from Baptist foreign missions, declaring it unchristian to treat slaveholders as sinners who were unfit for fellowship in missions. But while President Wayland worked with conservatives, he joined the 1854 Anti-Nebraska protest in Providence, Rhode Island, opposing the Douglas Bill, which permitted the extension of slavery into the western territory. Wayland voted for the new Republican party and told family and friends that the free states must vote together to free the country from "bowie-knives, bludgeons, and the lash." "The spirit of the North is up," he told his son, "and the day of truckling by compromise is . . .

---

12. Wendell Phillips Garrison, and Francis Jackson Garrison, *William Lloyd Garrison*, (New York: Century, 1885), 1:242–44.

13. Joseph Logsdon, *Horace White: Nineteenth Century Liberal*, 3–5, 8, 12, 28–31.

over forever. It is a blessing that Clay and Webster are dead." The anger of President Wayland had surely risen: he voted for Abraham Lincoln in 1860, applauded his victory, and predicted "God is about to bring slavery forever to an end."[14]

Wayland's Moral Philosophy was the most common source of Mugwump moral thought, but certainly not the single influence. The college text reflected a moral culture accessible in the Northeast without actually reading *Moral Science*. The Massachusetts Adamses, for example, had been learning those values at home since the American Revolution, when John Adams urged Abigail to teach the children to revere religion, morality, and liberty. They were taught that religion formed the morality and republican virtue upon which the future of the nation and the individual depended. Those ethics lessons were inculcated in the next generation by John Quincy Adams, who could be as harsh as Reverend Wayland in denouncing William Paley's permissive Moral Philosophy, writing in 1839, "Paley's Moral Philosophy, I wished they would burn it by the hands of the common hangman." For three generations, Adamses taught the Christian revelation of virtue and heaven or hell, with Charles Francis Adams Sr. attempting to teach it to Henry, Charles Francis Jr., John Quincy II, and Brooks.[15]

The only Wayland theme not taught in the Adams family would have been free-trade liberalism. The Whiggish family had advocated tariff protection for American industry, but so did Harvard. When Henry enrolled in Harvard College in 1854, the school had fallen under the influence of the Whig manufacturing elite who installed Reverend James Walker as Harvard president in 1853. And the new President Walker turned moral philosophy over to Francis Bowen, a cotton Whig compromiser who endorsed the Compromise of 1850, criticized Free-Soilers, and dropped the Wayland text. President Walker even ceased to talk like a moral philosopher. Where he had once taught that students had "a conscience, an innate inextinguishable sense of right," he now discouraged them from listening

14. John R. McKivigan, *The War against Proslavery Religion: Abolitionism and the Northern Churches*, 88–89, 122; Murray, *Francis Wayland*, 139–40, 143, 145–47; Smith, *Professors and Public Ethics*, 240.

15. Page Smith, *John Adams* (Garden City: Doubleday, 1962), 1:29, 219–20; John R. Howe Jr., *The Changing Political Thought of John Adams* (Princeton: Princeton University Press, 1966), 28–58; Charles Francis Adams, ed., *Memoirs of John Quincy Adams* (Philadelphia: J. B. Lippincott, 1876), 10:118–19; Greg Russell, *John Quincy Adams and the Public Virtues of Diplomacy* (Columbia: University of Missouri Press, 1995), 13–14, 67–95; Charles Francis Adams Sr., "Diary," Dec. 13, 1873, microfilm reel 85, Adams Papers, Massachusetts Historical Society (hereafter referred to as "Adams Papers").

to their consciences. "Conscience belongs to our emotional, and not to our intellectual nature," he said. "It is a sensibility and not a judgement."[16] Walker so evaded moral decision on the slavery question that he would not even vote in the presidential election of 1860. Perhaps Henry Adams was only slightly exaggerating when he claimed Harvard "taught little." He would have to fill out his liberalism from John Stuart Mill.

Young men who had earlier studied moral philosophy at Harvard did not suffer the confusion of the new teachers Bowen and Walker. Charles Eliot Norton, a 1846 Harvard graduate, stood firmly on moral principle in 1860, insisting that his friends continue "resolute maintenance of our principles,—the principles of justice and liberty." "This is no time for timid counsels," he said, even though he believed "we shall come at length to the rifle and the sword as the arbitrators of the great quarrel,—and I have no fear for the result."[17]

The thirty-three-year-old Norton had lived his moral philosophy for more than a decade before the election of Abraham Lincoln. As a young business executive he had organized the first adult night school in Massachusetts, recruiting a volunteer faculty of other young Harvard graduates, devoting two evenings a week to teaching ambitious individuals from the working class. In an article for the *North American Review* (July 1851), Norton urged that individuals should practice the virtue of benevolence with part of their labor, money, and thought for the good of society. Contributions to public education could prevent pauperism; investments in model housing could improve living conditions for the poor. All would gain when individuals practiced the virtues of benevolence and self-denial. In his essay on moral philosophy, *Considerations of Some Recent Social Theories* (1853), Norton declared that the future happiness of America depended on "prosperous and intelligent classes" practicing "Christian self-denial" and working against evils that threatened America. He urged that Americans work against slavery and other evils by "spreading and improving education, by laboring to throw open freely every opportunity for advantages that may be shared by all; by checking every injustice and every corruption; and, above all, . . . by endeavoring to carry into daily life and into common actions the spirit of Christianity."[18]

16. Howe, *Unitarian Conscience,* 297, 54, 283–84.
17. Sara Norton and M. A. DeWolfe Howe, eds., *Letters of Charles Eliot Norton,* 1:215–16.
18. Kermit Vanderbilt, *Charles Eliot Norton: Apostle of Culture in a Democracy,* 31, 38–42; Charles Eliot Norton, *Considerations on Some Recent Social Theories,* 141–45.

Norton's benevolence increasingly edged toward violence. His preference for war rather than compromise of moral principle was shared with his friend George William Curtis. To be sure, Curtis had less grounding in moral philosophy. The thirty-six-year-old Curtis had flunked his entrance exams to Brown and never attended the moral philosophy lectures of President Wayland, but values of a popular text were widely shared in the culture and Curtis managed to pick up the moral view of life from living in Brook Farm and from his New England Unitarian church. Curtis rose to fame as a popular writer and lecturer who turned his talents to the slavery issue in 1856, delivering an oration "The Duty of the American Scholar"— urging the educated to come out of their libraries and preserve liberty, speak for freedom, vote Republican, and prevent the expansion of slavery into Kansas. The object of republican government, Curtis stressed, had been the freedom of all individuals so each might improve and contribute to the development of society.[19]

While Curtis lectured for human freedom, Norton applauded his friend and, when the Civil War began, turned his literary talents to editing patriotic Loyal Publication Society propaganda and also the *North American Review*. Norton used his pen to preserve the moral foundation of the North and to impose a moral order of equality, freedom, and liberty on the South, which won him the applause of English moral philosopher John Stuart Mill.[20]

Norton encouraged other like-minded reformers. When a young British American, Edwin L. Godkin, came to Cambridge in pursuit of financial backing to create a weekly journal of moral opinion, Norton extended his friendship and recruited stockholders, pledging half of the necessary hundred thousand dollars for launching a new journal in New York with the most brilliant reform writer. Godkin, as editor, pursued amoral politicians as if it were a blood sport, indulging in a polemical style of caustic invective, witty sarcasm, exaggeration, and ridicule for impaling the enemies of civilization. The Godkin style endeared him to reformers while incurring permanent hatred from the victims.[21]

19. Charles Eliot Norton, ed., *Orations and Addresses of George William Curtis*, 1:3–35.

20. Vanderbilt, *Charles Eliot Norton*, 87; Norton and Howe, *Letters of Charles Eliot Norton*, 1:291; Charles Eliot Norton, "American Political Ideas," *North American Review* 101 (Oct. 1865): 550–66; Mill to Norton, Nov. 24, 1865, in J. M. Robson, ed., *Collected Works of John Stuart Mill*, 16:1119.

21. Rollo Ogden, ed., *Life and Letters of Edwin Lawrence Godkin*, 1:225–26, 236–37; Norton and Howe, *Letters of Charles Eliot Norton*, 1:283–84; after Godkin's first effort

While Godkin had not studied moral philosophy from Wayland's text, he shared liberal assumptions. The son of a Scotch-Irish Presbyterian minister, Godkin had learned his moral philosophy from the text of John Stuart Mill, who had written the best political economy text in the English language in 1848, recasting the "dismal" science back into the optimistic liberalism of Adam Smith. Individual liberty, Mill taught, with proper education and family planning, led to endless progress. The moral philosophy of Mill rested on utilitarianism, promoting the general happiness by following the golden rule of Jesus and helping others, practicing altruism. His readers acquired just as strong an obsession with character as did Wayland students. Selfishness might exist in markets, but no tolerance for greed existed in the moral philosophy of either Britain or America.[22]

The English-educated Godkin had entered journalism as a British war correspondent in the Crimean War of 1854, and then moved to America, reporting on the slave South and the American Civil War. A brilliant talker whose playful wit and affection made him a delightful table companion, Godkin became a close friend of the New York park designer, Frederick Law Olmsted, who made him a gift of his projected national weekly journal for the educated in America.[23] The *Nation* appeared in 1865, less religious than Wayland would have preferred, but an accurate reflection of American liberal thought. Young American liberals retained all the moral philosophy assumptions of Wayland except for the Christian faith. They too could read John Stuart Mill and drop religion. As Charles Francis Adams Jr. admitted, "I one day chanced upon a copy of John Stuart Mill's essay on Auguste Comte . . . that essay of Mill's revolutionized in a single morning my whole mental attitude. I emerged from the theological stage, in which I had been matured, and passed into the scientific."[24]

Adams had long heard praise of John Stuart Mill from his brother

failed, he joined abolitionist James M. McKim's drive to organize the *Nation;* see William M. Armstrong, ed., *The Gilded Age Letters of E. L. Godkin,* 29; Armstrong published three volumes on Godkin, but detested the editor for not being a twentieth-century liberal and found nothing, not even style, for unmixed praise; see William M. Armstrong, *E. L. Godkin: A Biography,* 50, 147.

22. Ogden, *Life and Letters of E. L. Godkin,* 1:3, 10–11; Pedro Schwartz, *The New Political Economy of J. S. Mill* (Durham: Duke University Press, 1972), 4, 193, 195; Stefan Collini, *Public Moralists: Political Thought and Intellectual Life in Britain, 1850–1930,* 61–62, 68–74, 107–8, 133.

23. Elizabeth Stevenson, *Park Maker: A Life of Frederick Law Olmsted,* 100, 241.

24. Charles Francis Adams Jr., *An Autobiography,* 179.

Henry, who had met the great man in London and recommended him as "the ablest man in England" and as a "high priest" of "our faith." This Mill essay treated Christianity as only a passing belief in the evolution of human thought from primitive to scientific. Mill encouraged Auguste Comte's religion of Humanity, which lacked a god but promoted moral restraint, teaching that altruism must predominate over egoism. Mill agreed a chief aim of education ought to be cultivation of benevolence. "No efforts should be spared," he said, "to associate the pupil's self-respect, and his desire of the respect of others, with service rendered to Humanity. . . ."[25]

"John Stuart Mill was our prophet," Godkin agreed. The British intellectual emerged as an international oracle in 1865. He won a seat in Parliament after a campaign so unpromising, it was said, that such tactics would not have given God Almighty a chance of being elected. Mill had refused to campaign or to pay a penny towards the cost of running, and, if elected, would refuse to support any local interests of the Westminster borough where he stood for election. Despite this unpromising campaign, Mill won on his intellectual reputation, and the victory gave him international prominence.[26]

A generation older than the Mugwumps, Mill had learned his radicalism at home. He had been educated in unbelief by a Scottish father who had reasoned his way free of any belief in God or any creator of God. The utilitarian father taught that Christianity harmed nations, concentrating minds on creeds and ceremonies rather than ethics and morality. The elder Mill preferred the virtues of classical Greek philosophers—justice, temperance, veracity, perseverance, and regard for the common good. The young John Stuart Mill grew up regarding conventional opinion in religion, morals, and politics as discredited in the more intellectual minds.[27] And young Americans felt liberated in being told old opinions had ceased to be reputable among the educated.

The unbelieving Mill asserted freedom of opinion in his *On Liberty* (1859) and freedom in the market in his *Principles of Political Economy* (1848), but he was very much a Victorian moralist. To be sure, he took another man's wife, Harriet Taylor, but he never advocated a moral laissez-

25. Henry Adams to Charles Francis Adams Jr., Jan. 30, May 1, 1863, in J. C. Levenson et al., eds., *The Letters of Henry Adams* 1:330, 350; John Stuart Mill, "The Positive Philosophy of Auguste Comte," in Robson, *Collected Works of John Stuart Mill*, 10:339, 268–91, 335, 337.
26. Ogden, *Life and Letters of E. L. Godkin*, 1:10; Michael St. John Packe, *The Life of John Stuart Mill*, 447–48, 479.
27. John Stuart Mill, *Autobiography*, 27–34, 167.

faire. He stood as the great advocate of altruism, Comte's new label for the old virtue of benevolence. Mill sought to improve human nature by education, persuading the "best men" to subordinate selfish feelings and promote the general good.[28]

Mill had held an unflattering attitude toward American greed before the 1860s, charging in his *Political Economy* that in America "the life of the whole of one sex is devoted to dollar hunting, and the other to breeding dollar hunters." But the American Civil War dramatically changed Mill to a friend of the Union. He came to the defense of the "good cause" of the North against the evil of slavery. He removed his offensive passage on American character from his sixth edition and worked to move English opinion behind the North.[29]

All American liberals read Mill, and many talked and corresponded with him. The shared passion for individualism and altruism permitted American students to move from Christian moral philosophy to secular liberalism with little change of values. A young Charles Francis Adams Jr. could switch from Christian to utilitarian ethics without changing his moral behavior. With the loss of faith, even the Unitarian Church retained too much dogma for Mugwumps, and yet their passion grew for character, benevolence, and morality.[30]

An explanation for the persistence of Mugwump morality is offered by the historian James Turner, who argued that President Francis Wayland and other evangelical ministers had inadvertently turned religion into morality. They intended only to adapt Christianity to a scientific culture, but their overemphasis on ethics created a science of morality that left students programmed to abandon belief in God when confronted by Charles Darwin's *Origin of Species* (1859).[31]

What was a moralist to think of God when told by Darwin that man had been the product of a wasteful, cruel competition of survival in which the sharpest claws and longest teeth always won? No kind, loving God would have permitted such an immoral process of suffering. Moralists trained in truth and evidence had to choose between science and belief.

28. Gertrude Himmelfarb, *On Liberty and Liberalism: The Case of John Stuart Mill*, 13, 82–83, 88, 106.
29. Packe, *Life of John Stuart Mill*, 423–26.
30. David D. Hall, "The Victorian Connection," *American Quarterly* 27 (Dec. 1975): 561–74; Norton and Howe, *Letters of Charles Eliot Norton*, 1:295, 2:430.
31. James Turner, *Without God, Without Creed: The Origins of Unbelief in America*, xiii, 82–85, 203.

God did not come up to moral standards. And the creation of species had not even needed God. Belief in science and morals erased belief in God.[32]

Agnosticism and unbelief emerged suddenly during the Civil War decade. "In 1850," according to Turner, "the intellectual ground of belief in God had seemed like bedrock; by 1870, it felt more like gelatin." Agnosticism had been virtually impossible for a thousand years in Western culture but now Charles Eliot Norton and other intellectual Americans began to dispense with God in the 1860s. Norton confessed to his British friend John Ruskin in the fall of 1869, "it does not seem to me that the evidence concerning the being of a God, and concerning immortality, is such as to enable us to assert anything in regard to either of these topics."[33]

The emotional unease following loss of faith led Mugwumps to grip even tighter the religion they had remaining, their morality, which had always been the essence of their moral philosophy. Professor Wayland had prepared them, without intending it, to be secular utilitarians. They had been taught to shape their behavior by the golden rule, behaving towards others as they would want others to behave towards them. Avoiding self-interest and pursuing the public good had been the religion of the college-educated and would continue as the religion of liberal intellectuals and the explanation of why they devoted so much of their lives to public morality.

Vigilance on moral issues imposed an orthodoxy on Mugwumps. E. L. Godkin, for example, almost became a casualty of reformer ethics during his first year of editing the *New York Nation*. In search of funding in protectionist Pennsylvania, Godkin promised to Philadelphia abolitionist James McKim that he would avoid the tariff issue and not make the *Nation* an advocate of free trade. Rumors of the amoral pledge impelled disgruntled stockholders to demand Godkin's resignation as editor. Godkin's "pledge" especially offended a Boston stockholder, Edward Atkinson.

Atkinson was an exception to the Mugwump's typical college preparation. Unable to attend Harvard when a family financial reversal sent him to work in a Boston dry goods store, the tall, burly Atkinson struggled to become a self-educated cotton textile manager; he studied his political economy from the texts of French popularizer Frederick Bastiat, and much of his tariff history from the English moralizer Harriet Martineau. With all the enthusiasm and energy of a self-made man, Atkinson sent letters

32. Ibid., 203–7.
33. Ibid., xi, 199.

of advice to the American presidents and articles to be published to the *Nation.* He really became indignant when Godkin declined to publish his free-trade essay because "a large amount of stock was subscribed in Philadelphia and some here, in the understanding that the *Nation* was not to be a free-trade paper." Atkinson turned Godkin's admission over to George Stearns, the principal *Nation* stockholder, who resented Godkin's independent coolness toward Radical Republicans, and they launched a movement to dump Godkin. Although Godkin won the stockholder majority, he had to promise to be a better liberal.[34]

With Godkin and liberal morality firmly in control, the weekly became independent of protectionists and radicals. It spoke for those public moralists who were to be labeled independents or Mugwumps in Gilded Age America. They had all deserted old parties—Whig and Democrat—to vote against slavery and for the Republican party of Abraham Lincoln. They did as their college ethics courses had taught—they voted for conscience and human freedom against the evil repression of individuals. If they lost the religious faith promoted by Wayland, they retained the ethics of his *Moral Science.* They agreed that education promoted progress in virtue and intelligence, that a conscience was a moral censor, and that the key to ethics was avoiding self-interest. Their indoctrination in moral character persisted except for the professor's assumption of a God in control of human progress. Substituting morality, science, and education for the hand of God, they vigorously pursued their benevolent duty to direct America toward virtue, civilization, and progress. They were educated to be public moralists. They feared no hell and promoted no religion, but they organized a generation of leadership, directing Americans to the good society.[35]

34. William M. Armstrong, "The Freedmen's Movement and the Founding of the *Nation,*" 708–26; Godkin to Atkinson, July 17, 1865, in Armstrong, *Gilded Age Letters of E. L. Godkin,* 39; for authors of the *Nation* articles, see Daniel C. Haskell, *The Nation Index, 1865–1917.*
35. For an international perspective on liberals, see Collini, *Public Moralists.*

2

The Money Question

Students of moral philosophy recognized a key currency question: would Congress follow the wisdom of political economists? Professor Francis Wayland, John Stuart Mill, and the other authorities agreed that markets in civilized nations had selected gold and silver for currency. Only these hard currencies, or bank paper exchangeable for them, were money. Government-printed paper money, to be sure, had been rejected and could never be real money because it always declined in value. The experience of history had repeatedly proven government paper to be a disaster for the morals and the pocketbooks of a people.[1]

But in the second year of the Civil War, the North's need to finance the struggle against the slave states created greenback paper money. Congressmen confessed that they were creating a train of evils: all values would shift as greenback inflation depreciated money in savings banks while raising the prices of real estate and hard assets; bad morals would be encouraged as debtors were tempted to pay obligations with cheap money; the boom of speculation would inevitably be followed by the bust of economic depression. Admitting that paper money was poison, Congress still thought greenbacks offered the best way to avoid bankruptcy and continue subduing the rebellion. Although Congress hated paper money in 1862, it still voted to print the greenbacks. "Reluctantly, painfully, I consent," Senator Charles Sumner of Massachusetts said, "and yet I cannot

---

1. Wayland, *Elements of Political Economy*, 299, 301, 312; for an introduction to the money question, see Walter T. K. Nugent, *The Money Question during Reconstruction* (New York: W. W. Norton, 1967), 52–64; Sidney Fine, *Laissez Faire and the General Welfare State: A Study in Conflict in American Thought, 1865–1900* (Ann Arbor: University of Michigan Press, 1956), 67–71.

give such a vote without warning the Government against the dangers from such an experiment."[2]

There was no organized opposition to the Legal Tender Act. Only a few bankers objected, while the poet and editor of the *New York Evening Post*, William Cullen Bryant, urged that President Lincoln veto the paper money legislation and prevent the ruinous cycle of inflation. "The evil of an irredeemable paper currency," Bryant said, "runs its course as certainly as the small-pox or any other disease."[3] Yet in a war against slavery, sacrifices were required, and moral philosophers would not oppose the government on greenbacks during the war.

The resulting inflation did double prices, creating enormous pain for people on fixed incomes, and yet the suffering reformers still felt good about their country at the end of the war. As the New York attorney and Columbia trustee George Templeton Strong confessed: "These four years have reduced me to something like pauperism. But I am profoundly thankful for them, nevertheless. They have given me—and my wife and my boys—a country worth living in and living for, and to be proud of. Up to April, 1861, it was a mean, sordid, money-worshiping country. . . ."[4]

The sacrifice of Northern citizens in the battle for abolition and freedom had endeared America to the moral philosophers. As Charles Eliot Norton boasted, the American political order had moved "in harmony with the moral laws of the universe." In 1865, American slavery ended with the Thirteenth Amendment, and Americans supported the ideal that all men were created equal as moral and responsible beings. The ideal of equality would certainly work itself into American institutions, reformers thought, because the war had proven that you could "trust in the fidelity of the people to the principles of justice, liberty and fair play."[5] A people who could be trusted to do the right thing about African American suffrage could also be trusted to abolish paper currency.

2. Wesley Clair Mitchell, *A History of the Greenbacks* (Chicago: University of Chicago Press, 1903), 51–69; Bray Hammond, "The North's Empty Purse," *American Historical Review* 67 (Oct. 1961): 1–18; *Congressional Globe*, 37th Cong., 2d sess., 1862, 800.

3. Parke Godwin, *A Biography of William Cullen Bryant*, 2:167–73; for ninety years scholars declared greenbacks a mistake, but twentieth-century Americans lost their fear of government paper, and Fritz Redlich, *The Molding of American Banking* (1951) approved; see, Robert P. Sharkey, *Money, Class, and Party: An Economic Study of Civil War and Reconstruction*, 33–34, nn. 70, 72.

4. Allan Nevins and Milton Halsey Thomas, eds., *The Diary of George Templeton Strong*, 4:56.

5. Norton to Miss Gaskell, Oct. 2, 1865, in Norton and Howe, *Letters of Charles Eliot Norton*, 1:285–87.

With all the optimism that characterizes victors at the end of a success-ful war, reformers were confident that government greenbacks were to be withdrawn from circulation. Secretary of the Treasury Hugh McCulloch, a New England–born banker whose sound money principles endeared him to reformers, promptly began taking greenbacks out of circulation and won congressional approval for his "contraction of the currency."[6]

Reformers understood that inflated prices were not solely the result of paper money. According to the quantity theory of money—prices rise as the quantity of money in circulation increases—gold and silver mining in the American West added to the currency supply and pushed up prices. Enormous government war purchases with borrowed money also raised prices, as did the lavish and reckless spending of the newly rich war contractors. Reformers understood the causes of price inflation and its remedy.[7] With government war buying ended and paper currency taken out of circulation, prices were certain to decline. All future threat of inflation would be ended once all the greenbacks were recalled and burned.

Classical monetary theory worked but reformer confidence in Amer-ican politicians did not. Once the post-war recession slowed business, employment, and manufacturing, Pennsylvania ironmasters and western commercial interests quickly denounced currency removal. Resistance to currency contraction increased until Congress repealed the Contraction Act in February 1868, with only $44 million retired out of a total of $400 million greenbacks.[8]

Confidence in Republican leadership vanished among reformers as politicians caved in to popular demands that greenback removal be stopped. Contraction had only begun to repair the inflation injury to members of the community who lived on fixed incomes—on salaries, rents derived from leases, interest on bonds and mortgages, and on annuities. Civil War inflation had deprived these people of half the amount of food, clothing, housing, and education previously within their means. They suffered months of personal austerity before prices hit their peak in 1865 and began to decline. Even three years later, in the fall of 1868, prices were still 50 percent higher than at the beginning of the war, and the

6. Sharkey, *Money, Class, and Party,* 56–74; Irwin Unger, *The Greenback Era,* 41; Hugh McCulloch, *Men and Measures of Half a Century* (New York: Charles Scribner's, 1888), 201–11.

7. Nevins and Thomas, *Diary of George Templeton Strong,* 4:52; E. L. Godkin, "Spend-thrifts and Prices," *Nation* 2 (May 29, 1866): 681.

8. Unger, *Greenback Era,* 43; Sharkey, *Money, Class, and Party,* 85–117.

New York Times was still saying, "there never was a time in our history in which the salaried classes—accountants, clerks, teachers, professors and clergymen—were so poor."[9]

The diary of George Templeton Strong records the injury felt by a man who lived on a fixed income and continued to suffer from 1865 to 1868. "I am maddened by the cost of living," Strong wrote. "Things tend from bad to worse, and I keep running behind every year, and cannot bear to give Ellie a serious talk about retrenchment—fewer little dinners, less opera, and so on." Lack of financial resources forced Strong to give up the little luxury of book buying. When his doctor urged him to take a vacation, he felt he could not afford the expense. He had hoped to be able to send his wife to Europe with her father, but he no longer had the means. Strong was forced to sell two one-thousand-dollar railroad bonds and he feared that he might also need to sell his house and library. "This process of depletion cannot be long kept up," Strong declared. "It is mere gnawing misery just now. Perhaps I shall be less wretched when an acknowledged pauper." Strong blamed the economic squeeze on the Legal Tender Act; for if the greenbacks had never been circulated, he could have been "less poor by some thousands."[10]

Strong may have shared financial interests with some reformers but he certainly was no representative figure. He refused to purchase stock in the *Nation* and never became a public leader for any of their reforms. Also, personal complaints about inflation injury did not characterize liberals; they were reformers, not complainers. Change of public policy engaged their attention, not preoccupation with self and suffering. Their moral philosophy directed them away from selfishness to benevolence.

The truth is that the leading reformers may not have suffered from inflation. They were capitalists rather than wage earners or bondholders. E. L. Godkin may have been closest to being just a salaried editor, but he had married money and was the major stockholder of the *Nation*. Other reform editors were part owners of their newspapers, and these capital investments would have kept in step with the rising prices. At least one editor, Horace White, speculated in whiskey futures and other capital investments. Edward Atkinson and David Wells invested in speculative ventures, including Kentucky iron and coal land, but they claimed to have

9. "Economy among the Middle Classes," *New York Times,* Nov. 9, 1868; for a chart of wholesale prices, see Don C. Barrett, *The Greenbacks and Resumption of Specie Payments, 1862–1879* (Cambridge: Harvard University Press, 1931), 97.
10. Nevins and Thomas, *Diary of George Templeton Strong,* 4:142, 166, 171, 275.

poor luck and were "bad speculators."[11] In short, we can neither be sure that greenback inflation harmed the interests of reformers as a group nor that their positions on the money question had anything to do with their economic self-interest.

A perfect illustration of the hard-money reformer going against his economic self-interest is found in the private diary of Charles Francis Adams Sr., who reluctantly became a debtor to protect his investment in Boston commercial property. "I never had any spirit of enterprise," Adams said, but on the advice of others he borrowed to erect a new store and office building, ending up with a debt of $111,000, twice what he had anticipated. Daily he suffered anxiety and depression. "The rest of my life is to be a struggle with debt," he moaned. "I am involved in a debt which I can hardly hope to repay. . . ." Yet Adams never changed his conviction that the first step towards reform "must be getting rid of the gambling in paper money." Rather than wishing to make his debts easier to pay with monetary inflation, Adams looked forward to the resumption of specie payments. "This paper fancy has been a delusion and a snare," Adams asserted.[12] Perhaps Adams never knew that currency contraction worked against his self-interest, but clearly he decided the great public questions without being controlled by his personal economic interests.

Reformers thought and wrote from the perspectives of moral philosophy and political economy rather than from economic self-interest. They complained that Congress, especially the western members, demonstrated an appalling ignorance of the science of political economy. Reformers had forgiven Abraham Lincoln's lack of culture and education but were now outraged that leadership had passed from the educated gentry class of the East to westerners who expressed contempt for education and boasted of their "ignorance." Senator Ben Wade claimed only seven days of schooling but still insisted that his natural reasoning was superior to the centuries of wisdom found in books. Western congressmen were shockingly ignorant of the most basic principles of political economy.[13]

11. Armstrong, *E. L. Godkin: A Biography,* 51, 91–92; Logsdon, *Horace White,* 97, 199; Edward Atkinson to David Wells, Mar. 30, 1880, Atkinson to C. P. Huntington, Sept. 1, 1881, Edward Atkinson Papers, Massachusetts Historical Society (hereafter referred to as "Atkinson Papers").

12. Charles Francis Adams Sr. "Diary," Feb. 2, 6, 7, 8, 15, June 21, 29, Nov. 6, 1878, reels 87, 88, Adams Papers.

13. "The New Type of Statesman," *Nation* 5 (July 4, 1867): p. 10; E. L. Godkin, "Why Political Economy Has Not Been Cultivated in America," *Nation* 5 (Sept. 26, 1867): 255.

Ignorance explained the barbarism of western politicians, but only bad character and the disruption caused by the Civil War could explain the emergence of such outrageous easterners as Benjamin F. Butler, upon whom a college education had been wasted. This former Democrat, who had nominated Mississippi's Jefferson Davis for the presidency in 1860, had used the Civil War to gain fame as the "Beast of New Orleans," accumulate personal riches from opportunistic commodity trading and seizure of southern gold, and then acquire a seat in Congress from Massachusetts. Ben Butler was a speculator and opportunist who sneered at the wisdom of political economy, suggesting that professors were as useless in politics as "a recluse old maid lecturing on how to bring up children." As a speculator who desired easy money, Butler gave no support to retiring the greenbacks or paying the national debt. "I am not for this generation paying all this debt," he said. "I think we have done our share when we contracted it. We ought to leave it to our children to do theirs by paying it." Butler even suggested paying off the national debt with greenbacks, to the outrage of all bondholders. The outrageous cynic and demagogue could amuse the voters, wave the Civil War bloody shirt, and win easy reelection in 1868, when the reformers sent in a man of principle, Richard Henry Dana Jr., to talk ethics and political economy. The distinguished Free-Soiler from outside the district could never compete for the votes of the working class against the racy, simple speech and buffoonery of Butler.[14]

With the reelection of Butler and the suspension of greenback contraction, reformers no longer believed the effects of the Civil War to have been entirely positive. While the nation had been crushing the evil of slavery, other evils had sprung up at home. Immigration might explain the corrupt Tweed Ring of New York City, but it could not explain the election of Butler and all the other rotten legislators, municipal authorities, judges, and politicians.

Reformers were restrained from attacking corrupt Republicans by the persistence of Reconstruction and African American civil rights, which reformers continued to support. If Republicans divided over economic issues, then Democrats might block freedom and equality for Southern

---

14. Samuel Shapiro, "Aristocracy, Mud, and Vituperation: The Butler-Dana Campaign in Essex County in 1868," *New England Quarterly* 31 (Sept. 1958): 340–60; Benjamin F. Butler, *Butler's Book,* 65, 952; Robert S. Holzman, *Stormy Ben Butler* (New York: Macmillan, 1954); historians Irwin Unger and Robert Sharkey credit Butler with being a "greenbacker" from conviction; my reading of his record is that this was only another opportunistic position.

blacks. Senator Charles Sumner of Massachusetts refused to criticize fellow Radical Republicans on currency issues. E. L. Godkin complained in the summer of 1867, "I shall thank God when the anti-slavery and negro question is fairly disposed of, and we can get a fair range at the corrupt rascals who grew up under it."[15]

Paper inflation seemed to have ruined not only the politicians but also the voters and the business community. Lawless speculators were thriving in both politics and commerce.[16] The rise of Ben Butler in politics had been accompanied by the rise of countless unscrupulous capitalists in the commercial world. Inflationary paper money seemed to have undermined the old business virtues encouraged by moral philosophers. In the earlier commercial America of Ben Franklin, the merchant made his way to fortune by "patient, steady plodding, through early rising, plain living, and small economies," E. L. Godkin said, but the practice of these virtues no longer brought success in the Civil War economy. In the new age of inflationary opportunity, the man who relied on traditional virtues was "left behind in the race." The prizes of commercial life were now won by "quickness of perception, activity, and courage." With "five out of six of the great fortunes . . . made rapidly, by happy hits, or bold and ingenious combinations," the old mode of working slowly up the ladder to business success by industry, frugality, punctuality, and integrity had fallen into disrepute. The opportunity to secure luxury quickly had turned the business community towards speculation.[17]

The gold and stock markets provided the more flamboyant means of speculative wealth, but all producers and holders of goods found it easy to make profits during the period of rising prices. It was well known that fortunes came from the oil fields of Pennsylvania and from contracts for the Army, Navy, Indian Department, and even the lighthouse service. Men suddenly grew rich in a multitude of occupations. "There were fortunes in whisky, in woolen or cotton goods, in bees wax, in quinine, in brimstone, and in all sorts of unexpected ways and things." And in any business, rising prices gave the advantage to the more adventurous, the more

15. Henry Adams to Charles Francis Adams Jr., May 8, 1867, in Levenson et al., *Letters of Henry Adams,* 1:533; Ogden, *Life and Letters of E. L. Godkin,* 1:300–301.
16. "True Radicalism," *Nation* 5 (July 18, 1867): 50–51; "Names in Politics," *Nation* 7 (Oct. 22, 1868): 324–25.
17. E. L. Godkin, "Commercial Immorality and Political Corruption," *North American Review* 107 (July 1868): 248–66; House, *Report of the Special Commissioner of Revenue,* 40th Cong., 3d sess., 1868, H. Doc. 16, 40–43 (microfiche 1372 no. 4, p. 1).

speculative debtor-entrepreneur. When certain of these entrepreneurs corrupted legislative bodies and courts of law with bribes, reformers protested: "Scoundrelism and effrontery in finance have so far succeeded in amassing millions and escaping punishment, that they have almost ceased to be regarded as disgraceful." The public conscience was thought by a Harvard moral philosopher to have become so diseased from "prolonged use of Paper Money" that bad money had done "even more harm to the morals of the country than to its commerce, its reputation, and its financial well-being."[18]

Preoccupation with the morals of the newly rich was explained by historian Richard Hofstadter as a status resentment, the complaint of a cultured gentry elbowed from power by the newly powerful.[19] Evidence of resentment is obvious in the reformer press criticism of the newly rich for lacking social graces. The new plutocrats were said to have spent their time making money and not to have taken the time to learn the social graces; having always eaten their meals hurriedly and silently, conversation at dinner was, for them, almost an unknown art. Their dinners were characterized by "barbaric magnificence" and the lack of "taste, intelligence, and mutual respect." This "flash society" had attempted to shove aside the old leaders of culture. The *New York Times* complained that "a certain pack of vulgar upstarts," who had made money by usury, by watering stocks, or by robbing the public treasury, were attempting to lead society. To overthrow these new men, the *New York Times* prescribed an unwritten "Social Charter" to purge the newly rich by refusing to recognize as passports to social distinction the largest diamonds, the most conspicuous box at the opera, or a showy yacht. Further, the charter would prohibit the preference of a "mere heavy purse" to "brains, or public service, or exalted character, or attainments in science, in letters, or in art."[20]

While resentment of the newly rich was clear in the 1860s, reformers acted from more virtuous motives than status resentments. Surely real crime and real immorality were reason enough to oppose greenbacks and the newly rich. When young Henry Adams, the descendant of two presidents, began his career as a reform journalist in the 1860s,

18. Francis Bowen, *American Political Economy* (New York: Charles Scribners, 1870), 342.
19. Richard Hofstadter, *The Age of Reform*, 137–43.
20. C. A. Bristed, "A Society for Improving the Condition of the Rich," *Nation* 1 (Sept. 28, 1865): 399; "New York Society," "Evening Entertainments," *New York Times*, Jan. 1, 1872, p. 4, Jan. 2, 1874, p. 4.

he published one article on the Legal Tender Act blunder and another on Jay Gould and Jim Fisk, two poor boys who became rich villains in the Civil War inflation.[21] Gould was born on a poor hill farm in Roxbury, New York, but moved from the tannery business to railroad speculation. His partner in vice, Jim Fisk, began as a peddler, rose to the jobbing business in Boston, and moved into high finance at the close of the war. These speculators joined forces with Daniel Drew, a director of the Erie Railroad, and together managed such spectacular operations as looting stockholders and purchasing special legislation to legalize their fraud. They bought a white marble palace in the style of European aristocrats and purchased Pike's Opera House on Eighth Avenue, which supplied Fisk with women enough for a "permanent harem." With shameless ostentation he rode around New York with his "batch of harlots." It seemed to Henry Adams that not even Honoré de Balzac or Alexandre Dumas had ever depicted an instance of social mobility as striking as the rise of Gould and Fisk to the top of New York society. Yet the reformer's real outrage protested the corruption of law and culture. Fisk and Gould used their fortune to purchase the law. They bought judges, political bosses, and the New York state legislature. The best of lawyers, David Dudley Field, a law reformer and brother of Supreme Court Justice Stephen J. Field, willingly entered their pay. Even President Grant associated with Gould and Fisk while they attempted to exploit their contact to corner the gold market. In 1869 the speculators conspired in a gigantic bull action, driving the price of gold from $140 to $163 before government sales stopped the "Black Friday" conspiracy and ruined countless speculators.[22]

Henry Adams understood Fisk and Gould as the worst examples of an exceptionally corrupt time created by greenback inflation. As he explained, "the civil war in America, with its enormous issues of depreciating currency, and its reckless waste of money and credit by the government, created a speculative mania such as the United States, with all its experience in this respect, had never before known." Reform would require a restoration of the "moral and economical laws" so that rascals

21. Henry Adams, "The Legal-Tender Act," *North American Review* 110 (Apr. 1870): 299–327; for the self-interest interpretation of Adams, ignoring moral philosophy, see Brooks D. Simpson, *The Political Education of Henry Adams.*

22. Henry Adams, "The New York Gold Conspiracy," reprinted in Charles Francis Adams Jr. and Henry Adams, *Chapters of Erie* (Ithaca: Cornell University Press, 1956), 101–36.

and their corporations could no longer "override and trample on law, custom, decency, and every restraint known to society. . . ."[23]

Greed and corruption were never regarded as typical of business ethics in nineteenth-century America. Fisk and Gould may shock no twentieth-century readers, but Victorians knew the normal marketplace not as a Hobbesian war of all against all but, instead, as a moral endeavor governed by restraint and the golden rule. Henry Adams may have had no market experience, but Edward Atkinson of Boston reflected two generations of experience when he declared the notion of commerce as greed and exploitation "so far from the truth as to be almost absurd." His merchant father told him that in forty years of business, bad debts had not come to "fifty cents on each one hundred dollars' worth of goods sold." The cotton textile manufacturer knew that commerce "would be difficult if the great mass of men did not intend to live fairly and deal fairly with others." And the English moral philosopher, John Stuart Mill, said that civilization rested on trust. "If we cannot trust each other's word we may as well go back to the woods," Mill said. Greenbacks had weakened the American sense of obligations and restraint; they had to go.[24]

The elimination of greenbacks proved more difficult than the reformers imagined. A return to the settled wisdom of political economy should have been easy, but the paper money remained in circulation for half a century. Not until 1913 and the Federal Reserve Act were the greenbacks finally abolished. To be sure, the paper currency could be exchanged for gold after the specie resumption of 1879, but even a gold-backed currency could not be trusted by reformers, since Congress controlled the supply. So long as politicians were empowered to create paper money, reformers said, no person could go to bed at night knowing what his property would be worth the next morning. Politicians would be tempted to inflate the money supply so long as they had the power to print currency.

Inflation troubled reformers for their entire adult lives, uniting them behind the hard-money position of civilization and morality. A Mugwump simply could not approve of inflationary currencies any more than he could permit human slavery. Both government policies violated liberal beliefs in absolute individual rights of life, liberty, and property.

23. Ibid., 135–36.
24. Edward Atkinson, *The Industrial Progress of the Nation* (New York: G. Putnam, 1890), 383–84; Mill to Charles Eliot Norton, Sept. 24, 1886, in Robson, *Collected Works of John Stuart Mill*, 16:1443–48; for an explanation of capitalism as a civilizing force, see Thomas L. Haskell, "Capitalism and the Origins of Humanitarian Sensibility."

When Congress altered property rights by tampering with the money supply, it turned government from a neutral enforcer of standards into a coconspirator of economic groups, inviting a Hobbesian struggle in which even life and liberty might be sacrificed. The destruction of one absolute right threatened the safety of all. Inflationary currencies changed property values and personal ethics for the worse, and so Mugwumps stood with John Stuart Mill, Francis Wayland, and liberalism against monetary inflation until Congress finally relinquished its money-making power to the Federal Reserve Board in 1913.

3

The Tariff

American manufacturers posed as patriots in persuading Congress to double taxes on foreign competition during the Civil War, creating steep price increases that consumers would never have permitted except for the crisis. During a war for preservation of the Union, as well as freedom, the erection of protective tariffs could be defended as a patriotic revenue producer.[1] Just as Northern citizens reluctantly consented to greenbacks, so did they consent to 47 percent tariffs. But once the fighting ended, consumers paying inflated prices expected tariffs to be quickly reduced, if not abolished.

The moral case against protective tariffs had been made long ago by Professor Francis Wayland. The president of Brown University reasoned in his *Elements of Political Economy* (1840) that if manufacturers were given fortunes by congressional legislation, those unearned profits had been taken from the American consumers. No moral law sanctioned a society to steal from one class to give to another. Society had no moral right to destroy wealth of consumers by forcing them to pay more. Wayland further stressed that economic arguments for tariff protection had no logical merit. Reflecting Adam Smith's criticism of mercantilism, Wayland thought legislative interference with markets could never add to a nation's wealth, but could certainly subtract. While all people and nations gained from free exchange conducted upon the principles of benevolence, all could lose if trade were manipulated as a selfish war for personal advantage.[2]

---

1. Frank W. Taussig, *Tariff History of the United States*, 160–67; Representative Samuel S. Cox testified that the conference committee in 1864 had promised to repeal the temporary war tax as soon as internal taxes were removed; see *Congressional Globe*, 41st Cong., 2d sess., Mar. 28, 1870, 2240.
    2. Wayland, *Elements of Political Economy*, 140–60, 167–91; Joseph Dorfman, *The Economic Mind in American Civilization* (New York: Viking Press, 1946), 2:758–59.

Wayland's free-trade theory gained practical support from the textile manufacturer Edward Atkinson, who knew the costs for New England cotton spinners. This Boston manufacturer, who purchased Egyptian cotton and thus paid import duties, found his costs for manufacturing thread higher than the thread maker in Britain whose government added no tariff duties to raw materials. To eliminate handicaps for American manufacturing, Atkinson advocated gradual repeal of all custom duties except for those purely revenue tariffs on tea, coffee, alcohol, tobacco, sugar, and spices. This English system of raising revenue, he said, would damage neither manufacturers nor consumers.[3]

Political economists in American colleges admitted the truth of free-trade liberalism. Even Harvard protectionist Francis Bowen conceded, in his *Principles of Political Economy* (1856), that he believed in the principle of laissez-faire, which meant "God regulates . . . by his general laws, which always, in the long run, work for good." Insisting on one exception to the general law, Bowen promoted a temporary protective tariff for the "infant industries" of America. To be sure, even the dean of contemporary British economists, John Stuart Mill, had conceded protection for "infant industries," but Mill, who corresponded with a number of American reformers, insisted that U.S. industry had ceased to be infant and deserved no protection from competition. In 1866 Mill declared, "the manufacturing parts of the United States—New England and Pennsylvania—are no longer new countries; they have carried on manufactures on a large scale, and with the benefit of high protective duties, for at least two generations; their operatives have had full time to acquire the manufacturing skill in which those of England had preceded them."[4]

If some disagreement about the wisdom of tariff protection existed among reformers before the Civil War, that debate quickly ended after 1865. Free trade, or more precisely revenue rather than protective tariffs, became the reformer position in the great tariff debates that were staged in Congress every two years. The campaign to return to a revenue tariff is best explained by relating the story of David A. Wells, the slight, stooped,

3. Edward Atkinson, *On the Collection of Revenue* (Boston, 1867); Harold Francis Williamson, *Edward Atkinson: The Biography of an American Liberal*, 73–78.

4. Francis Bowen, *The Principles of Political Economy* (Boston: Little, Brown, 1856), 23, 493. Mill to Horace White, Feb. 26, 1866, reprinted in John Stuart Mill, *Principles of Political Economy*, 614–15.

bespectacled scholar of forty who became the central tariff reformer for the Mugwumps.[5]

Wells reflected a New England reformer background including a youthful heresy of Whig tariff protection. He was born in 1828 at Springfield, Massachusetts, to a puritan Congregational family engaged in retail business. When the father failed as a dry-goods retailer, the mother took the children home to live with her wealthy manufacturing parents who were, of course, advocates of protection from foreign-manufactured paper. Living with his protectionist grandfather gave Wells a pro-tariff· outlook. When he studied moral philosophy at Williams College in the 1840s, Wells proved resistant to free-trade instruction from Francis Wayland's *Elements of Political Economy*. Then, after earning a second degree from the Lawrence Scientific School at Harvard in 1851, Wells became a science writer living in Philadelphia, where he joined the protectionist circle of Henry C. Carey, the chief apologist for Pennsylvania ironmasters and heavy-industry protection. The book publisher and iron capitalist had no standing with academic economists, but Carey's wealth, intellectual energy, and social standing gave him enormous support from industrialists and, for a time, from Wells, who claimed to be his disciple.[6]

Wells stood out as one of the few reformers who actually sought government office. Of course he pretended to be a virtuous republican and not a pursuer of office, yet Wells made himself a financial expert, created a new position in the Treasury Department, and then secured that position for himself. The Wells strategy began during the Civil War when the declining public credit made government bonds difficult to sell. So Wells wrote his thirty-nine-page pamphlet, *Our Burden and Our Strength* (1864), examining the American ability to repay a $3 billion war debt. His use of statistics demonstrated America's terrific growth rate: nineteenth-century population had grown by 35 percent each decade, while national wealth had grown at 10 percent per year. America could indeed carry its debt more easily than Britain had successfully managed

---

5. For intellectual agreement in the colleges, see Dorfman, *Economic Mind in American Civilization,* 3:80, and Fine, *Laissez Faire and the General Welfare State,* 47–95; the best work on Wells remains Herbert Ronald Ferleger, *David A. Wells and the American Revenue System, 1865–1870.*

6. Ferleger, *David A. Wells,* 2–5; Dorfman, *Economic Mind in American Civilization,* 2:808–9; John Stuart Mill regarded Henry Carey as important enough to refute in *Principles of Political Economy* (1871), see Robson, *Collected Works of John Stuart Mill,* 3:919–21.

its even worse debt at the end of the Napoleonic Wars. Wells persuaded the Loyal League of Boston to distribute two hundred thousand copies of his pamphlet in America and in Europe, while he himself sent copies to countless politicians, editors, and leaders of opinion. He then created the demand for an official Treasury Department commission of outside experts to study tax policies necessary for managing the national debt, and then he lobbied for his own appointment to that Special Commission of Revenue in 1865.[7]

Wells, the scientist, collected statistical data on the $3 billion in obligations, the existing taxes, then considered revenue systems of major European countries. He concluded that experts recommended the British system for collecting huge amounts of revenue without damaging the development of a nation. The British system had grown out of Manchester manufacturing complaints of a thousand taxes on foreign produce, which forced food prices upwards for workers and increased raw materials costs for manufacturers. The path to national prosperity, the Manchester party persuaded Parliament, eliminated tariffs on food and materials used by English manufacturers. And Wells insisted that America follow that British wisdom and stop taxing raw materials.[8]

Wells called attention, in his January 1866 report, to a dramatic example of evil results created by unwise American taxes. Five thousand employees of umbrella factories in Philadelphia and New York were being driven out of their jobs by thoughtless taxes. War excise taxes had been levied not only on domestic umbrellas but on every part purchased for use in the assembly of those umbrellas. The imported fabric cover for the umbrella incurred an especially stiff tariff duty. The combined taxes drove the price of American-made umbrellas far above any imported umbrellas. All internal excise taxes had to go, Wells said, as well as all tariffs on raw materials used in American manufacturing. If workers and manufacturers were to prosper and pay their share of the national debt, then government policies must stop driving up their prices.[9]

7. Ferleger, *David A. Wells*, 15–21; Hugh McCulloch to Wells, Mar. 24, 27, 1865, microfilm reel 1, 45–46, David A. Wells Papers, Library of Congress (hereafter referred to as "Wells Papers"); the other experts were Stephen Colwell and S. S. Hayes.

8. House, *Revenue System of the United States*, 39th Cong., 1st sess., Jan. 29, 1866, H. Doc. 34, 5–13; for a persuasive essay that Britain was turned to free trade not by capitalists but by politicians concerned with increasing the nation's income, see William D. Grampp, "How Britain Turned to Free Trade," *Business History Review* 61 (Spring 1987): 86–112; A. C. Howe, "Free Trade and the City of London," *History* 77 (Oct. 1992): 391–410.

9. Ferleger, *David A. Wells*, 13–16.

A second example of unwise taxation ruined the American book-publishing business. According to Wells, the public schools of America were purchasing *Webster's Spelling Book* from British publishers. American publishers could not compete because of the excise taxes and the tariff on imported paper, the raw material for books. Thoughtless taxation had doubled the American publisher's costs for manufacturing a book. And the solution, Wells said, was not to add even higher tariffs on foreign books, but to remove "the shackles from industry" by abolishing all taxes that damaged American manufacturing. Excise taxes and import duties on raw materials must go.[10]

Wells entered the Treasury Department in the summer of 1865 as a moderate protectionist. In Washington, studying federal taxation, he met a wider circle of reformers who were in agreement with classical economics. One new acquaintance, Horace White, editor of the *Chicago Tribune,* corresponded with John Stuart Mill and added "Free Trade" to his earlier antislavery slogan of "Free Soil, Free Labor, and Free Speech." The thirty-two-year-old editor of the leading Radical Republican paper in the West joined the Chicago Board of Trade in organizing the Free-Trade League in January 1866; it would lobby for tariff reduction to be pushed to the head of the Republican agenda. To be sure, western editors, politicians, and interests were naturally hostile to a protective tariff because they had little or no manufacturing to protect. Morality and self-interest are not always totally separable, however much Mugwumps liked to assert that they could be separated. But White believed that he came to free trade though moral philosophy and not self-interest. In New York City, prominent editors also supported free trade, with considerable support from the importing and merchandizing center of America that had been irritated by tariffs. Wells met journalist E. L. Godkin of the *New York Nation,* and from the *Evening Post* he met the old editor William Cullen Bryant, president of the American Free-Trade League, and the new editor, Charles Nordhoff. In addition to the voices of these liberal editors, an intellectual capitalist from Boston, Edward Atkinson, shared the data he was collecting for his own revenue paper before the American Social Science Association.[11]

The Boston textile manufacturer took tariff reform so seriously that he had attempted to oust editor E. L. Godkin of the *Nation* for insufficient moral principle. The reader will recall that as a financial investor in the *Nation,* Atkinson had felt entitled to submit his own essay "Free Trade

10. Ibid., 16–17.
11. Ibid., 195–96, 253.

and Protection" for publication in the new journal. Godkin declined to publish the article, explaining that "a large amount of stock was subscribed in Philadelphia and some here, in the understanding that the *Nation* was not to be a free trade paper." An indignant Atkinson trumpeted his opinion that Godkin had pledged away his moral virtue to the Philadelphia protectionists and should be removed from the editorship. Godkin barely survived the purge by affirming his own belief in free trade and promising to never support tariff protection.[12]

The bumptious textile manufacturer and liberal reformer worked diligently to convert Wells, and by the summer of 1866, Wells conceded: "I have changed my ideas respecting tariffs & protection very much since I came to Washington & am coming over to the ground which you occupy. I am utterly disgusted with the rapacity and selfishness which I have seen displayed by Pennsylvania people & some other sections on this subject."[13]

In speaking of Pennsylvania greed, Wells revealed his Mugwump assumption that citizens should act for the general good. Under his cover of scientific inquiry, Wells retained moral philosophy assumptions about promoting the general welfare with his tariff policy. His campaign to eliminate taxes on raw materials sought to permit American manufacturers to produce more cheaply for home and export markets, creating more wealth and employment for all Americans. But the Pennsylvania iron manufacturers refused to see pig iron as having this proper role in the national economy. Even if high prices for this raw material drove up costs of other finished iron products manufactured from pig iron, Pennsylvania men did not care. They wanted obscene profits guaranteed to them by unreasonably high tariffs on foreign pig iron. To be sure, Congressman William D. "Pig Iron" Kelley also claimed to be speaking for the general welfare, but it was impossible to take seriously a man who described Wells as "in the pay" of English capitalists.[14] Wells and greedy capitalists simply spoke different moral and tariff philosophies.

In the tariff debates, education and culture were generally on the side of free trade. Wells's superior, Secretary of the Treasury Hugh McCulloch, shared reformer beliefs in free trade and sound money. On the other side were largely provincial interests, especially the pig-iron men

12. E. L. Godkin to Edward Atkinson, July 17, 1865, Godkin to Charles Eliot Norton, July 22, Aug. 24, 1865, in Armstrong, *Gilded Age Letters of E. L. Godkin*, 39, 41, 53–54; Armstrong, "Freedmen's Movement," 708–26.

13. Ferleger, *David A. Wells*, 154.

14. William D. Kelley, *Speeches, Addresses, and Letters* (New York: Greenwood, 1969), 273, 289.

of Pennsylvania who insisted that their war tariffs be continued and even increased. Pennsylvania iron industrialists were also heavy users of borrowed money who supported greenback inflation, violating both the money and the tariff principles of classical economics. The personal greed of the manufacturers offended the scholarly Wells, but he was enough of a politician to continue pretending to be one of them for three more years, writing to their protectionist leader, Henry C. Carey, as late as 1869: "I think the High Tariff people ought to stand with me for endeavoring to stand between them and destruction. I know what elements are preparing all over the country to make war on the principles of protection. Nearly all the pens and tongues which contended against slavery are ready to begin the conflict. All moderate men can be rallied round my position, which is simply one of moderation, yet distinctly protective."[15]

Behind his pretense of being a moderate protectionist, Wells confided to his free-trade friends in 1867 that he shared their beliefs and would be coming out soon. "The time has not however come for me to distinctly avow my sentiments," he told Professor Arthur L. Perry of Williams College. "I am accumulating a store of facts, which private individuals could not obtain. . . . To provoke opposition now, would probably close the door to some important investigations; so for the present I must work on silently." But he wanted his free-trade friends to not be silent; Wells organized them into a newspaper campaign. He told Professor Perry, "I have arranged with Atkinson, Raymond of the *New York Times,* Nordhoff of the *Post,* and several writers & Editors of the West that during the next six months there shall be an earnest discussion of the subject kept up through the papers; and a more vigorous attempt than ever made to change public sentiment, and my main object in writing to you now is to ask that you will commence at once and write every week an article for the *Springfield Republican* on the subject—short and pithy. Ridicule will I think be fully as effective as argument."[16]

Wells did use his government position to research and demolish the protectionist defense that had shifted from pretending to protect infant industries to pretending to support high wages of American workers. Wells investigated the validity of those claims during a three-month trip to Europe in the summer of 1867, and he learned that countries with the

15. McCulloch, *Men and Measures,* 237–42. Wells to Carey, Jan. 1869, reprinted in Ferleger, *David A. Wells,* 237.
16. Wells to Perry, Mar. 11, 1867, reprinted in Ferleger, *David A. Wells,* 180–81.

highest protective duties—Italy and Russia—paid the lowest wages. Wells could now prove that protection had little or nothing to do with high wages; the real key to higher wages, he insisted, was higher productivity.[17]

These free-market ideas could easily have been picked up at a dinner with the Cobden Club in London, where Wells dined with political, business, and intellectual leaders committed to international free trade. The Cobden Club began as a commemorative body in 1866, observing the first anniversary of the death of the parliamentary leader of the free-trade movement. Richard Cobden, the Manchester calico manufacturer, had organized the Anti-Corn Law League and had gone to Parliament to force Great Britain to commit to free trade. Cobden's friends used the club to publish statistics supporting the cause and to influence countries to move toward free markets. The club especially cultivated sympathetic American leaders, honoring Congressman James A. Garfield and writer Ralph Waldo Emerson with honorary memberships in 1866, and David A. Wells in 1867.[18]

With encouragement from British free traders and from Edward Atkinson, James Garfield, and all the editors and professors, Wells determined to come out against protection in his third report. Of course he feared that coming out as a tariff liberal might damage him politically, but he optimistically assumed that a man never lost by "adhering boldly to the truth." In fact, Wells fully expected to be nominated by President Grant as Secretary of the Treasury in 1869; all his friends agreed he was the most qualified.[19]

The 1869 *Report* boldly declared that economic growth and rapid recovery from the war had been accompanied by two critical problems that created an unfair economy in which *"The rich become richer and the poor poorer."* The troubles were the greenback currency and the unreasonable tariff, which had ballooned beyond revenue needs to add an average of 48 percent to product prices. As an example of the unjust tariff, which needlessly enhanced prices, Wells pointed to pig iron, which Congress had given more than a 50 percent profit. The cost of producing a ton of

17. Ferleger, *David A. Wells*, 192–99.

18. Donald Read, *Cobden and Bright: A Victorian Partnership* (London: Edward Arnold, 1967), 241–42; Allan Peskin, *Garfield: A Biography* (Kent, Ohio: Kent State University Press, 1978), 289–90; for Cobden, see Wendy Hinde, *Richard Cobden: A Victorian Outsider.*

19. Ferleger, *David A. Wells*, 220–24, 249–50; Fred Bunyan Joyner, *David Ames Wells: Champion of Free Trade*, 89–90.

pig iron was a mere $24, but tariff protection from foreign competition permitted the Pennsylvania men to sell for $37 to $42 a ton, giving them an unnecessary $7 to $10 profit and costing consumers millions. The greed of the pig iron industry led other manufacturers to demand their increased profits until even the producers of "bibles and ice" were demanding protection.[20]

Friends of free trade congratulated Wells on his work, telling him "Your report is . . . the most important & valuable state paper ever produced in this country on any financial or economical subject. The high tariff gentry will never get over it." Wells had created the "most important paper as to Finance since the days of Hamilton." "This Report will be our Bible in our future onslaughts on the Monopolists." "There is more of the science of Political Economy in it than any official paper ever issued in this country." "You will be the *Cobden* of America . . . you will win for our country the same victory and honor he won for his."[21]

But protectionists launched a barrage of criticism when the *Report* appeared. The angry Henry Carey sent thirteen long letters to the *New York Tribune* challenging Wells and concluding with the insult that he must have been bribed by British gold. To avoid libel laws, Carey took the precaution of putting the accusation in the form of a question: why was it that Wells's report was so in accordance with the wishes of British capitalists who were accustomed "to distribute money so freely among those of our people who are supposed to be possessed of power to influence public opinion?" Horace Greeley's *Tribune* furthered the fraudulent charge, asserting: "We do most surely believe that the scope and drift of Mr. Wells's late Report was influenced by the money of foreign rivals. . . ."[22] The hostile criticism dashed all hope of joining the Grant cabinet.

Wells never really had a chance of entering the Grant cabinet. In an age of military leaders, he was too much the mild-mannered scholar. Even his friends admitted he possessed no "popular manners" or executive style.

20. *Report of the Special Commissioner of the Revenue,* 40th Cong., 3d sess., Jan. 5, 1869, Doc. 16, 1–11, 47, 69–76.
21. Horace White to Wells, Dec. 24, 1869, reel 1, 412; F. A. Walker to Wells, Dec. 30, 1869, reel 1a, 448; A. L. Perry to Wells, Dec. 31, 1869, reel 1a, 449–52; Amasa Walker to Wells, Jan. 8, 1870, reel 1a, 467–68; Elihu Burritt to Wells, May 14, 1869, reel 1, 343–44, Wells Papers.
22. *New York Tribune,* Mar. 9, 1869, p. 5, Mar. 23, 1869, p. 4; Ferleger, *David A. Wells,* 224–21, 249–50, 274–302; Joyner, *David Ames Wells,* 89–90; Glendon G. Van Deusen, *Horace Greeley: Nineteenth-Century Crusader,* 329.

The editor Henry J. Raymond of the *New York Times* objected that Wells lacked the personal qualities essential for financial leadership. Raymond wanted "fighting qualities" in a Secretary of Treasury sufficient to push through free trade and specie resumption. Wells was "too amiable," too inexperienced in the practical politics of managing men. The cabinet position would be beyond Wells's management abilities. So although Wells never enjoyed universal support of the free-trade press, he suffered bitter opposition of protectionists who would even prevent the extension of his Special Commissioner position in 1870, leaving Wells with only a role as leader of liberal reform.[23]

Wells still had his following. The young journalist Henry Adams boasted proudly to his British friends that he was a lieutenant of David A. Wells in the battle for tariff reform and for the creation a new party. "I have had a political convention of half the greatest newspaper editors in the country in my rooms," Adams reported, "where the world was staked out to each of us and . . . the foundations of Hell were shaken." Meeting in the Washington apartment were Wells, former Secretary of the Treasury Hugh McCullogh, E. L. Godkin of the *Nation*, Joseph R. Hawley of the *Hartford Courant*, Charles Nordhoff of the *New York Post*, Horace White of the *Chicago Tribune*, and Edward Atkinson.[24]

These friends of reform had propagandized popular opinion for more than a year and were now ready, in 1870, to force Congress to reform the tariff. Getting a reform bill through Congress proved more difficult than they had imagined. Only fifty Democrats could have been classified as free traders, along with only three or four western Republicans. Representative S. S. Cox of New York reminded the Congress that all experts from Adam Smith through Francis Wayland had objected to protective tariffs as legalized robbery. "All the colleges—nearly all the learned people— are of that way of thinking," Cox said. The "grasping protectionists" were guilty of a "shameless breach of faith and honesty." But after three months of debate, Congress moved against the advice Wells had given them. The protectionists kept all their high tariffs and reduced duties on tea, coffee, wines, sugar, molasses, and spices, which Wells had hoped would fund a revenue tariff. The only victory was a symbolic two-dollar

23. H. J. Raymond to Horace White, Nov. 17, 1868, reel 1; Francis Lieber to James Garfield, June 7, 1870, reel 1a, Wells Papers.
24. Adams to Charles Milnes Gaskell, Mar. 28, Apr. 29, 1870, in Levenson et al., *Letters of Henry Adams* 2:68–69; Logsdon, *Horace White*, 180.

reduction on the Pennsylvania pig iron and its obnoxious Representative Kelley.[25]

Perhaps reformers should have been disappointed in the failure of tariff reform, but they were cheered by the debate, which they thought had ended congressional complacency, awakened public attention, and rudely shaken party lines. Reformers assembled in New York in the fall of 1870, with the officers of the Free Trade League, to plan the future. Wells and eastern reformers insisted on splitting with the Republican party, which had given them virtually no support. But the western reformers, led by Horace White of the *Chicago Tribune,* insisted that they must continue trying to work with the dominant Republican party. White trusted Republican House leader James G. Blaine, who pretended to be one of them and had offered to let reformers control the House Ways and Means Committee. Western reformers also hesitated to organize a new party because they were less enthusiastic about the hard-money demands of eastern reformers. Western demands for credit and easy money made monetary contraction unacceptable to western voters. Reformers were enthusiastic about tariff and civil service reform but were not yet ready to endorse burning the greenbacks. So the 1870 meeting adjourned short of organizing a new party, unless the understanding with Blaine failed to work out. If the Republican Congress failed to live up to Blaine's promises, then the western reformers promised to join the easterners in calling for a convention to organize a reform party.[26]

Disappointment with Blaine's broken promises was inevitable. By the next spring, Horace White no longer believed the Speaker to be worthy of trust or honor. Congressman Garfield agreed, writing to Wells, "I don't think B. has acted altogether like a white man about it. He will bear a good deal of watching."[27]

And so by 1871, reformers had completely lost faith in the possibility of reform within the Republican party. The Democratic organization remained too tainted with treason, racism, and debt repudiation for reformers to join. So formation of a third party offered the only hope for immediate change. Western reformers and the Wells crowd of

25. *Congressional Globe,* 41st Cong., 2d sess., Mar. 28, 1870, 2240–49, 2557; Henry Adams, "The Session," *North American Review* 111 (July 1870): 44–46; Taussig, *Tariff History,* 179–80.

26. Adams to J. D. Cox, Nov. 28, 1870, in Levenson et al., *Letters of Henry Adams,* 2:91–92; Logsdon, *Horace White,* 182–83.

27. Garfield to Wells, May 20, 1871, reel 1a, 769, Wells Papers.

eastern reformers regarded the tariff as their major cause. They united in agreement with the John Stuart Mill sentiment that protection was "an organized system of pillage of the many by the few. . . ."[28] Free trade was essential to raise the incomes of Americans, establish a moral economy, and change a corrupt political system.

28. For tariff as the major Ohio concern, see Michael E. McGerr, "The Meaning of Liberal Republicanism: The Case of Ohio," *Civil War History* 28 (Dec. 1982): 308; Mill to Charles Loring Brace, Jan. 19, 1871, in Robson, *Collected Works of John Stuart Mill,* 17:1798.

4

Civil Service Reform

The central problem for liberal reformers was the collapse of public morality. "The moral law had expired," Henry Adams complained. The eighteenth-century fabric of moral principles had broken down. Reformers blamed the collapse on government corruption. All their solutions— hard currency, free trade, and civil service reform—were efforts to end government-permitted stealing. While civil service has been called their main reform, only for Carl Schurz or George William Curtis would this have been true. Creating a professional, nonpartisan civil service was no panacea but did promise to go to the root of decay in public morality by killing the patronage system that funded political machines and professional politicians. The hope of reformers was to take government workers out of politics, and politicians out of patronage corruption, ending the spoils system that controlled elections, preventing citizens from selecting officials committed to good government.[1]

The Republican party especially seemed to have degenerated into a patronage machine rewarding its campaign workers with municipal, state, and federal jobs and then assessing them 2 to 4 percent of their salary, and much of their time, for keeping party bosses in control of party and elected office. Republican politics of the Grant administration had become a spoils system promoting graft and bribery rather than public virtue. Democratic politics in state and local government were even worse with

1. Richard Hofstadter called it "their chief issue, civil-service reform," in his *Anti-intellectualism in American Life* (New York: Alfred Knopf, 1963), 174; and John G. Sproat called it their "panacea" in *"The Best Men": Liberal Reformers in the Gilded Age,* 257; Thomas Haskell rejected the "inconsequential panacea" thesis, explaining that the reform contributed to giving America professional management; see Thomas L. Haskell, *The Emergence of Professional Social Science,* 117–21; for the collapse of moral law, see Henry Adams, *The Education of Henry Adams,* 280; for criticism of the moral collapse argument, see Mark Wahlgren Summers, *The Era of Good Stealings,* x.

Boss Tweed's machine plundering New York City and selling justice in the courts. "Corruption in our legislative bodies, our great corporations, and now even in the state judiciary, and in the sheriff's office, has at last reached a stage that must produce revolutionary action if no legal remedy can be found," New York City diarist George Templeton Strong wrote in 1869. "The dishonesty of every man in public office is a violent presumption, and universally recognized as such."[2]

Every town knew a politically appointed postmaster but New York City watched a federal Custom House on Wall Street where a thousand political appointees inspected and taxed all foreign goods coming though the port. The reputation of federal treasury collectors for graft and inefficiency went back a generation but, like most federal agencies, had grown during the Civil War. And David A. Wells, as Special Revenue Commissioner, calculated that $25 million might have been lost annually to the federal treasury. Importers were both exploited and exploiters of the system, giving bribes and underpaying their tariffs in return. Here, a crony of President Grant could draw a larger income than the president and not even find it necessary to show up for work.[3]

Reformer outrage about corruption reverberated for a hundred years —until the 1960s—and then ceased to be given credibility. Historians Richard Hofstadter and Ari Hoogenboom shifted the story around to the old denials of spoilsman Benjamin F. Butler: reformers were just "outs" who wanted to get "in."[4] Historians embellished the politician's old story with a fresh interpretation: reformers were a declining elite frustrated because their class had been pushed out of office by new Americans. The new story contained only a grain of truth but created a perverse understanding that liberal reform should be viewed as the reactionary backlash of a declining group. Such an interpretation, based on status, ignored the moral-philosophy background of reformers, failed to find any important civil service reformer who sought office through the reformed merit system, and seemed to suggest that political corruption really should not have created public outrage.

2. Paul P. Van Riper, *History of the United States Civil Service*, 30–56; Nevins and Thomas, *Diary of George Templeton Strong*, 4:245–46.

3. Ari Hoogenboom created a great book, except for the thesis. If one ignores his status-resentment explanation for reformers, *Outlawing the Spoils* is an outstanding history; Ari Hoogenboom, *Outlawing the Spoils: A History of the Civil Service Reform Movement*, 17–18, 25, 102–3.

4. Hoogenboom, *Outlawing the Spoils*, ix; Hofstadter, *Anti-intellectualism in American Life*, 172–91.

Civil service reform actually required neither self-interest nor politics of resentment to gain the support of American intellectuals. Every civilized country in the Western world had enacted competitive examinations, appointments based on merit, and tenure for good behavior as the standards for public employment. College-trained Americans looked to Europe, and especially to England, for solutions to public problems. Great Britain had enacted civil service reform in the 1850s, and so Harvard-trained Senator Charles Sumner proposed a copy of British legislation in 1864, and, the following year, Brown University–trained Representative Thomas A. Jenckes introduced a second civil service reform bill.[5] Needless to say, these elected Republicans were neither political "outs" nor victims of declining status.

The "father" of civil service reform, Representative Jenckes, studied moral philosophy with President Wayland at Brown and then became a patent attorney and a manufacturer in Rhode Island. Jenckes introduced his first reform bill in December 20, 1865, and explained with great candor that he and his committee proposed to withdraw the public service from being used as an instrument of "party patronage." The legislation proposed to "dig up, root out, and throw aside any, every, and all kinds of 'patronage' in appointments to the public service." Patronage had "no place in a republic" but was a relic of corrupt paternalism where one owed service to superiors rather than to the voters of the republic. The old system of giving public jobs as a reward for political partisanship had given America the most vicious system of customhouses in the civilized world, Jenckes said. Our civil service had become a refuge for "the idle, the corrupt, the ignorant, the dissolute, or the dishonest," who, he said, were given even less respect than the public school teachers. Jenckes would improve the character and efficiency of the civil service by making character and merit the standards for employment and retention. In two House reports, Jenckes educated his colleagues on civil service reform in Great Britain, France, and Germany, inserting the John Stuart Mill defense of competitive examinations for the British government, as well as a history of the civil service in America and interviews with American public employees on how poorly our system operated.[6]

5. Ari Hoogenboom, "Thomas A. Jenckes and Civil Service Reform," *Mississippi Valley Historical Review* 47 (Mar. 1961): 636–58; Hoogenboom, *Outlawing the Spoils*, 10–15.

6. *Congressional Globe* 39th Cong., 2d sess., Jan. 29, 1867, 837–38, 840; House, *Civil Service in the United States*, 39th Cong., 2d sess., 1867, H. Rept. 8; *Civil Service of the United States*, 40th Cong., 2d sess., 1869, H. Rept. 47.

The real question, to be sure, is not why Jenckes introduced civil service reform, but why liberal reformers joined in support. Status historian Ari Hoogenboom offered an easy answer, relating that Henry Adams had told his brother in 1869, "I can't get you an office." And Hoogenboom concluded: "With their ambitions thwarted, the Adams brothers forsook the conventional methods of political advancement and espoused civil service reform." But the evidence does not really support this claim that Henry Adams's motives were those of a disappointed office seeker. Two years before, he had told his brother, Charles Francis Adams Jr., "I never will make a speech, never run for office, never belong to a party."[7] Such a denial does not prove that Adams never desired high office, but he did act on that denial and sought a career in journalism, not politics.

Henry Adams may be cleared of personal political ambition but not of resenting professional politicians. Evidence of Adams's class resentment is clearly expressed in his journalism. While contrasting Attorney General Ebenezer Hoar with secretary of the Treasury George Boutwell, Adams explained that although the two Republicans came from the same congressional district, "Yet one was the type of that narrow political morality which has obtained so general a control of America,—the product of caucuses and party promotion; the other was by birth and by training a representative of the best New England school, holding his moral rules on the basis of his own conscience, indifferent to opposition whether in or out of his own party, obstinate to excess. . . . Judge Hoar belonged in fact to a class of men who had been gradually driven from politics, but whom it is the hope of reformers to restore. Mr. Boutwell belonged to the class which has excluded its rival, but which has failed to fill with equal dignity the place it has usurped."[8]

Reformers clearly sought to retake government from the new politicians, but not as mere political "outs" seeking to regain office and power. Adams described their class struggle as including not only "birth," but

7. Hoogenboom, *Outlawing the Spoils*, 63. Henry Adams to Charles Francis Adams Jr., Nov. 16, 1867, in Levenson et al., *Letters of Henry Adams*, 1:557; Charles chose railroads and capitalism rather than political office. The one brother who chose politics, John Quincy, did not join his brothers in civil service reform. Henry declared his intention of a literary life in the 1858 Harvard "Life-Book," see Edward Chalfant, *Both Sides of the Ocean: A Biography of Henry Adams, His First Life, 1838–1862*, 97; for a differing interpretation that Adams was a "pompous little ass" who "itched for office," see Simpson, *Political Education of Henry Adams*, 29–31, 118.

8. Henry Brooks Adams, "Civil Service Reform," *North American Review* 109 (Oct. 1869): 556; Hoogenboom, *Outlawing the Spoils*, 67–69.

also "training," "conscience," and "morality." Boutwell represented the other class because he had been neither a college man nor a Free-Soiler; he had been a Democrat, which had never been the party of morality. Hoogenboom would have us believe Secretary Boutwell was really an equally enlightened administrator, but the reformers knew Boutwell to be a close associate of spoilsman Benjamin Butler, another former Democrat, for whom he had campaigned in the last Massachusetts congressional election. Just as Butler hooted at all reform, so Boutwell took no interest in moral philosophy, greenback contraction, free trade, or retaining Special Revenue Commissioner David A. Wells in the Treasury Department. Boutwell practiced partisan politics and held on to office while Hoar was forced from the Grant cabinet for refusing to make patronage Republican appointments.[9]

Politics seemed, to the Adams brothers, to have returned to corruption such as their father, Charles Francis Adams, had faced when the Whig party refused to deal with human slavery and forced him to become a Free-Soiler and a Republican. Now Henry and Charles Francis Jr. found the Republican party lapsed from moral ideas and in the grip of professional politicians corrupted by the patronage system. Adams ethics taught loyalty to principles rather than to party, so the brothers attacked the corrupt spoils practice that had transformed the Republicans from a party of reform.[10] Reformers were primarily interested in a restoration of virtue, but their enemies—the spoilsmen—and the later status historians, mistook their action as a campaign for power, office, and self-interest.

The editor of the *New York Nation,* Edwin L. Godkin, never sought political office and yet eagerly fought corruption. He believed New York government to be "a blot on our religion and our civilization." This editor, an immigrant himself, said the source for New York corruption had been immigration: "a swarm of foreigners . . . ignorant, credulous, newly emancipated, brutalized by oppression, and bred in the habit of regarding the law as the enemy," had been pandered to by unscrupulous Democratic politicians. On the national level, Republican

9. For Boutwell's own story, see George S. Boutwell, *Reminiscences of Sixty Years* (Boston: McClure, Phillips, 1902); and for the reformer distaste, see Unger, *Greenback Era,* 190–92.

10. For the breakdown of moral principles, see Adams, *Education of Henry Adams,* 280–81; Adams, "Civil Service Reform," 443–75; and a more recent perspective, Summers, *Era of Good Stealings,* x, 22, 93–95.

politicians had been corrupted not by immigration but by the spoils system, Godkin said. Godkin believed that he had started the reform movement.[11]

The campaign for civil service reform became serious in 1869. Before, the unsettled Reconstruction issues of Andrew Johnson and African American rights had dominated public discussion, but with these problems cleared away by the inauguration of President U. S. Grant and Republican support for the Fifteenth Amendment, the patronage scandal could be pushed before public opinion. The force behind the new public campaign was the Social Science Association, a Boston group of abolitionists and reformers who had formed in 1865 to collect data, develop common ground on the great social problems, and guide the public to the best solution. The Bostonians organized civil service meetings in Boston and New York for Representative Jenckes to promote his reform legislation. Then, the Social Science Association brought George William Curtis into the reform movement.[12]

Curtis possessed star quality as a reform speaker, having won fame in the abolition debate. No one thought he was the brightest, but he possessed style and stage presence, as well as a feeling for the popular pulse. As personal friend Charles Eliot Norton explained: "His principles are as firm & clear as the glass tube, but his feelings & his opinions as to modes of action & courses of policy vary with the popular weather. This makes him an excellent & useful political writer & actor in such a country as ours & at such a time as this. He is not a statesman of the first class,—of whom there are none in America just now—but one of the first of the second class."[13]

Curtis asked the New York audience assembled by the American Social Science Association in October 1869 to restore that republican virtue to the civil service which President George Washington had established. Good citizens must end the demoralization of America, Curtis said, which resulted from the bartering of civil service positions for party politics. Civil service positions must once again be awarded on qualifications of knowledge, ability, and morality. To be sure, tests for morality did not

11. Ogden, *Life and Letters of E. L. Godkin*, 1:300–301, 2:40–41; E. L. Godkin, "The Government of Our Great Cities," *Nation* 3 (Oct. 18, 1866): 312–13.
12. For the origins of social science, see Haskell, *The Emergence of Professional Social Science*, 91–101; Hoogenboom, *Outlawing the Spoils*, 55–56.
13. Norton to Godkin, Feb. 1, 1867, E. L. Godkin Papers, reprinted in *Outlawing the Spoils*, 34.

exist, but ability could be measured, and those examinations could end the spoils system for appointments and preserve the national character.[14]

Congress absolutely refused to endorse competitive examinations. Any requirements of merit were halted by Congress even when Representative Jenckes explained his intent as promoting honesty, frugality, and efficiency, rather than killing partisan patronage. Jenckes said he just wanted to weed out the "rogues, thieves, or incapables." Candid Republicans replied that patronage must remain a permanent political procedure. The more demagogic even waved the bloody flag by labeling reform an aristocratic scheme to ignore disabled Civil War soldiers in favor of the college-educated elite. Representative John Peters of Maine bellowed: "If the bill passes, what are you going to do with the thousands of crippled soldiers all over this country who . . . may not be able to pass the highest examination . . . to spell all words with strict correctness, or construct the most grammatical sentences. . . . ? Will you take the civilian and college-bred boy, who can most easily pass such examinations . . . and put aside the soldier who yet can discharge the duties of the office well enough . . . ?"[15]

Even so limited a civil service reform bill as Senator Lyman Trumbull's proposal that congressmen stop recommending and pressuring the president on appointments failed to win senatorial consent. Certainly, congressmen agreed that patronage requests were "onerous, burdensome, distasteful, and intolerable," but they were not about to give up their right to assist a qualified voter from home in getting a job interview with the president.[16]

The four civil service bills drafted by Trumbull, Jenckes, Carl Schurz, and Henry Wilson had no chance of gaining a congressional majority. The best that supporters of reform could manage was a rider, attached to an appropriation bill, authorizing President Grant to appoint a committee and to establish rules for examining applicants. The resulting commission, headed by George William Curtis, laid down the reformer's rules—competitive examinations and no political assessments of government workers—that President Grant declared would apply beginning January 1, 1872.[17]

14. Charles Eliot Norton, ed., *Orations and Addresses of George William Curtis*, 2:3–28.
15. *Congressional Globe*, 41st Cong., 2d sess., May 3, 1870, 3223.
16. Ibid., 3d sess., 669, 782.
17. For the Curtis commission rules, see Norton, *Orations and Addresses of G. W. Curtis*, 2:29–80; Hoogenboom, *Outlawing the Spoils*, 85–87, 17.

Reform seemed to be winning, but Grant actually had pulled a political deception. The Curtis rules only bound Grant's administration, but he had no intention of being bound by reform rules. He had fired the two cabinet officers who refused to permit patronage appointments in their departments. And he had replaced an honest collector of the New York Custom House with the spoilsman Thomas Murphy. Grant's only purpose for the civil service commission was to win reformer votes for his reelection in 1872. And only a few reformers were fooled.[18]

The danger of American political corruption frightened not only American liberals but their British moral philosopher mentor. John Stuart Mill regarded the spoils system as "far more serious" than tariff protection that only wasted enormous sums of American money. On the other hand, Mill said, corruption of politicians, "saps the very roots of free government & the triumphant success of villainy by corrupting your legislatures & even the bench of justices, cannot go on without demoralizing the whole nation."[19] The concern of Mill came not from a jealous office seeker, or one declining in status, but from a public moralist worried about American democracy.

18. Hoogenboom, *Outlawing the Spoils,* 88, 110; Thomas C. Reeves, *Gentleman Boss: The Life of Chester Alan Arthur* (New York: Knopf, 1975), 56; Armstrong, *E. L. Godkin: A Biography,* 127–30.

19. Mill to Charles Loring Brace, Jan. 19, 1871, in Robson, *Collected Works of John Stuart Mill,* 17:1798.

5

The Liberal Republican Party of 1872

When Henry Adams shifted from Washington journalist to Harvard history professor in the fall of 1870, his plans included the creation of a new political party. He would edit, in his spare time, the *North American Review,* turning it into a central organ of the new party. Adams confided to friends that his retirement from Washington had by no means thrown him out of politics. "On the contrary," he said, "as editor I am deeper in them than ever, and my party is growing so rapidly that I look forward to the day when we shall be in power again as not far distant. Two or three years ought to do it."[1]

The new Adams party assembled supporters of David A. Wells from the press and the Free Trade League for a New York City conference in November 1870. Editors E. L. Godkin of the *Nation,* Charles Nordhoff and William Cullen Bryant of the *New York Evening Post,* Samuel Bowles of the *Springfield Republican,* Horace White of the *Chicago Tribune,* and William Grosvenor of the *St. Louis Democrat* agreed that history moved towards their currency, tariff, and civil service reforms. The old parties had ignored their issues, so the time had come for a new party of principles. Recent elections in Missouri had demonstrated that a new party could win.[2]

The Missouri reform leader was Carl Schurz, a Prussian immigrant who had become a United States senator. The son of a village schoolmaster, he had been a student at the University of Bonn when the republican revolutions of 1848 swept Europe. Schurz assumed a leadership role in the student rebellion that would have marked him for prison had he

1. Levenson et al., *Letters of Henry Adams,* 2:85–89.
2. Ibid., Adams to Jacob D. Cox, Nov. 28, 1870, 2:91–92.

not escaped to France. After a daring reentry into Prussia to liberate his captured professor a from Berlin prison, Schurz married a German heiress and immigrated to the American West. As a literate immigrant who had quickly mastered English, Schurz was welcomed in the 1850s by a new Republican party seeking to win German-American voters away from the Democratic party, which had traditionally welcomed immigrants. As a liberal opposed to slavery, Schurz moved German Americans into the Republican party and restrained the party from making Know-Nothing slanders against immigrants. In repayment for helping Abraham Lincoln win in 1860, Schurz received a patronage position as minister to Spain and then a political appointment as a Brigadier General in the Union army.[3]

After the war, Schurz bought into the *St. Louis Westliche Post* and made himself the Missouri spokesman for German Americans and their choice for the United States Senate. Schurz entered the Senate in 1869 intending to make civil service reform and not ethnic politics his specialty. Schurz knew the high civil service standards of his native Prussia and the principles of New England independents with whom he had cooperated since the 1850s. His inevitable collision with President Grant over patronage endeared him to the reformers as did his liberal objections to the protective tariff.[4]

The Missouri reform movement began in the fall of 1870 when the state Republican boss, Charles D. Drake, dictated his slate of candidates, endorsed President Grant, and called for continued disfranchisement of former Confederate sympathizers. Schurz, whose life was one of resisting tyrants, regarded Drake as an opportunistic boss who could not to be trusted to pursue the common good. Drake had even been a Democrat until the second year of the war and then converted to Radical Republicanism, seeking power by becoming the most bitter enemy of Democrats. Schurz led the walkout from Drake's Republican convention, nominating a slate of Liberal Republican candidates for state office and endorsing civil service reform, free trade, and an end to disfranchisement of Missouri Democrats. Democrats rallied to the reform standard and overturned radical control of Missouri in the 1870 election.[5]

3. Carl Schurz, *The Reminiscences of Carl Schurz*, 2:3–17, 65–70; Hans L. Trefousse, *Carl Schurz: A Biography*, 3–44, 48–61, 73–74, 88–116.

4. Trefousse, *Carl Schurz*, 150–74; Joseph Schafer, ed., *Intimate Letters of Carl Schurz* (New York: Da Capo Press, 1970), 475, 477; Claude Moore Fuess, *Carl Schurz: Reformer*, 167.

5. William E. Parrish, *Missouri under Radical Rule*, 4–6, 264–67; Thomas S. Barclay, "The Liberal Republican Movement in Missouri," 3–78.

If the new party could win in Missouri, then reformers might also defeat President Grant's attempt for a second term. The president had wrecked his reputation with reformers in less than two years, preferring the company of spoilsmen Simon Cameron and Ben Butler. Grant ousted his two cabinet civil service reformers—Jacob D. Cox and Ebenezer Hoar—because their refusal to tolerate patronage spoils angered congressional leaders. Rather than devoting himself to specie resumption, tariff, or civil service reform, President Grant had thrown his weight behind the speculators and opportunists advocating annexation of San Domingo. Under Grant's leadership, the Republican party had failed to move beyond waving the bloody Civil War shirt. Cynics would say that Grant had just become a smarter politician, cutting ties with reformers to gain support from the Republican Congress. But such practical politics were evidence to reformers that Grant lacked character and had to go.[6]

In rejecting Grant and the Republican party, reformers did not so much abandon African Americans as simply move on from their victory over slavery. Blacks had achieved freedom and equal legal rights. With the Civil War amendments written into the Constitution, reformers wanted local government restored to the South. Home rule, to be sure, would lead to a restoration of rule by former Confederates, who made up two-thirds of the Southern population. Reformers did not wish to see blacks denied their rights but neither did they want to see the white South turned into an Ireland, a hostile people ruled by foreign force. The Irish in the 1870s still accused their British oppressors of genocide, of being responsible for two million Irish deaths in the potato famine. In the turbulent colony, young men seemed in a constant plot of nationalistic Fenian uprisings, police assaults, and landlord murders. No one could say that outside occupation had worked well in Ireland. As republican believers in the moral theory that good government results more from the virtue of the people than from laws of the legislature, reformers did not want to destroy any Southern white sense of responsibility for local preservation of order. The American tradition had included a sense of personal responsibility to preserve safety, law, and order. If Americans began to look to Washington for law and order, the habit of self-government might be fatally weakened. E. L. Godkin explained, "it is not in the goodness of the laws that the success of republican institutions on this continent has been due, *but to*

6. "Politics," *Nation* 11 (Sept. 29, 1870): 200; J. B. Hodgskin, "The Political Situation," *Nation* 12 (Mar. 9, 1871): 152; Summers, *Era of Good Stealings,* 185–96; James Ford Rhodes, *History of the United States from the Compromise of 1850* (New York: Macmillan, 1919), 7:1–13.

the habits of the people, and notably to the habit which every man has of looking on the work of local police as his personal affair. This is the distinctive feature of American society."[7]

The goal of republican government, as understood by reformers, was not equality but liberty and civilization. Republican principles required that slavery be destroyed and African Americans be given votes to protect their freedom. The *Nation* and most liberals began supporting black voting in 1865. But these same reformers insisted that to continue depriving Southern white men of their votes and their "natural influence" as the educated class, offended both civilization and republicanism. If anarchy were to be avoided and the constitutional requirement of local self-government upheld, Southern whites must be restored to power and the relations of the black and white races left to be adjusted by time. Those who wished the African American citizen well, according to Godkin, "should preach to him incessantly the lesson of self-reliance and self-deliverance; should spend all they can for books and maps and teachers for him; and as little as possible on gaseous lectures about his political rights. . . ."[8]

To put independent Republican attitudes towards African Americans in context, only one reformer was so fearful of race as President Lincoln, who talked of colonizing blacks outside America. Only Jacob D. Cox, antislavery Republican, Civil War general, and Ohio governor, refused to support suffrage and talked of moving blacks into a separate homeland on the south Atlantic coast, perhaps Florida, in 1865.[9] Governor Cox did not persist in his misguided opinion and his letters never even mentioned race by 1870. A member of the Henry Adams circle who had resigned as Grant's Secretary of Interior rather than permit patronage to control his appointments, Cox wrote the civil service reform paper for Adams's *North American Review* and the new party. His real interest, however, was economic liberalism and tariff reform. Cox joined other independent Republicans and Democrats to sign the 1871 call for a Cincinnati convention to launch a new Liberal Republican party.[10]

7. "A Look Before and After," *North American Review* 108 (Jan. 1869): 263; Gamaliel Bradford, "Congressional Reform," *North American Review* 111 (Oct. 1870): 330–31; E. L. Godkin, "Police Duty," *Nation* 12 (Apr. 27, 1871): 284–85; for Ireland in the 1870s, see W. E. Vaughan, ed., *A New History of Ireland,* vol. 5 (Oxford: Clarendon Press, 1989).
8. E. L. Godkin, "What Shall We Do With the Negro?" *Nation* 7 (Nov. 12, 1868): 386–87.
9. Robert D. Sawrey, *Dubious Victory: The Reconstruction Debate in Ohio,* 36–37.
10. Earle Dudley Ross, *The Liberal Republican Movement,* 47; Richard Allan Gerber, in an otherwise useful article, "The Liberal Republicans of 1872 in Historiographical Perspective," 46, claims Earle Ross "magnified the tariff reform issue out of proportion,"

While Henry Adams's magazine laid out the principles of the new party, William Grosvenor organized the correspondence and address book. A Massachusetts native, Yale graduate, and Civil War colonel, Grosvenor had become a journalist in Missouri at the end of the war. An active political participant in antiradical Missouri politics, Grosvenor turned full time to politics after losing his editorship of the *St. Louis Democrat* in 1871. He boasted of building a national organization among friends of reform that would extend down to the township level and ultimately swallow up the Democratic party. What he intended to do with political power is less clear. Certainly he had demonstrated liberal credentials by publishing an antitariff treatise, *Does Protection Protect?* (1871), but Grosvenor appears to have had more of a political than an economic agenda. His ties and friendship were with fellow-Missourian Gratz Brown, whom he backed for the presidency. While he was on cordial terms with the free-traders before the Cincinnati convention, afterwards he would be regarded as a traitor who sold out principle for Greeley and Brown.[11]

The liberal reformers of 1872 were clear headed in their issues. Their declaration of principles for promoting general amnesty for ex-Confederates, tariff for revenue only, civil service reform, and resumption of gold convertibility for greenbacks had been laid out in Henry Adams's articles in the *North American Review*. But reformers never thought so clearly about an adequate presidential candidate, because republican moralists all believed that no man should seek the presidency. The same quality that enabled reformers to get together on the issues—refusal to promote self-interest—prevented any of them from announcing and campaigning for the presidency.

Discussion and correspondence among the reformers produced a leading candidate, Henry Adams's father—Charles Francis Adams Senior. The elder Adams, son of one president and grandson of another, had been quiet and scholarly but pushed himself into abolition work, writing, speaking, and organizing against the evil of slavery. Adams would not promote himself for public office, but when nominations were pressed on him, he did his duty, serving in the Massachusetts legislature in the

but had no manuscript sources to back his tariff interpretation. The Wells Papers offer an abundance of correspondence that speaks of little but the tariff issue; see J. D. Cox to Wells, July 22, 1871, Mar. 16, 1872, reel 2, 840–47, 960–62, Wells Papers.

11. Henry Adams to D. A. Wells, Jan. 17, 1871, reel 1a, 665–66, Wells Papers; Barclay, "Liberal Republican Movement," 21:277–78; Edward Atkinson to Wells, Sept. 23, 1875, reel 3, 1898, Wells Papers.

1840s. The Free-Soil candidate for the vice presidency in 1848, Republican congressman in the secession crisis of 1860–1861, and then ambassador to Great Britain, he became the most acclaimed American diplomat of his time. He then led President Grant's negotiating team in Geneva to press Civil War naval claims against the British. In meetings with the president, Adams concluded that Grant was "an ignoramus" and "utterly incompetent," but Adams had no burning desire to be president himself. In fact, his children knew better than to tell him that he was being publicly mentioned as a presidential possibility. Adams first heard the news on March 18, 1872, from a Democratic post office politician, and was offended that he should be expected to risk "contamination with the dirt of electioneering for place." "I am in no humor to cultivate such people," Adams wrote in his diary, "so I told him that I had not a word to say. If the country called me into its service, it was my rule to obey. . . . But I would take no mere party nomination, neither would I spend my time in running after a Jack o'lantern. . . . I could never bend to make my way through the mass of political prizefighters who block up every avenue to the highest station."[12]

In the following weeks, Adams continued to be irritated by each mention of his name in the press and to look forward to his scheduled return to the Geneva negotiations as an escape from politics. Every thought of running for president gave him "a shudder." The fearful but clear-thinking Adams had no illusions about winning: running for office would require a "furious campaign," in which reputation would be "blackened" and defeat certain, because no overwhelming public demand for change existed in 1872. Of course, he admitted to himself that his vanity had been flattered by talk of his nomination for the presidency. But he did not want to run and would not cooperate with those who wanted him to seek the nomination. "I shall soon be free from that annoyance by leaving the country," he wrote in his diary.[13]

David A. Wells pursued a campaign of persuading Adams to declare his willingness to be a candidate. Announcing his intention of nominating Adams through letters to the Adams sons, Wells asked John Quincy II, the Democratic politician, to let him know Adams's "sentiments and principles." A second letter, to Charles Francis Jr., the Railroad Commissioner, requested that he get his father to issue a statement of principles and

12. Charles Francis Adams, "Diary," Feb. 23, Mar. 18, 1872, reel 84, Adams Papers.
13. Ibid., Mar. 30, 1872.

permit the sons to go to Cincinnati to represent and negotiate for his nomination.[14]

The Adams sons warned against seeking any pledges from their father. As America's negotiator in the Geneva talks with Great Britain, the elder Adams had an official position that he regarded as above politics, and he believed that any intrigue of his for party ends would be "disgraceful." So strongly did the old man regard his civic virtue that his sons not only could not go to the Cincinnati convention, but Charles Francis Jr. also had to ask to withdraw his name from the list of those endorsing the convention. The sons had no right to compromise their father's official position. They could tell Wells that their father abhorred paper money and protection, believed in local self-government, and had a great sympathy for Carl Schurz's career, but they could not speak for their father.[15]

The Adams nomination seemed so certain that Roscoe Conkling, a Republican, sent a competing offer of the vice presidency if Adams would promise to accept a Republican offer (and take himself out of consideration by the new party). Adams, of course, refused to make any promises to Republicans, just as he refused to give the Liberal Republicans any commitments.[16] Any bargaining for an unwanted office or campaign was repulsive to Adams.

Wells rashly wrote directly to Adams, drawing a distinction between asking him to seek the office and asking only that he permit his friends to know his opinions and his willingness to accept their presidential nomination. Yes, Adams had the support of the *Springfield Republican, New York Evening Post,* former Secretary Jacob D. Cox, and Senators Lyman Trumbull and Carl Schurz; he was "the one most likely to unite the conservative elements of the country," but Wells needed to know if Adams could endorse the principles of the Cincinnati call and if he would accept the nomination if chosen.[17]

Adams never precisely refused, but he did pen a letter with such an unwilling tone as to prevent his nomination. He would authorize no one to negotiate for him; he dismissed the principles of the movement as only platitudes and gave not a single word of encouragement for the Liberal

14. Ibid., Apr. 10, 1872.
15. J. Q. Adams to Wells, Apr. 10, 1872, reel 2, 975–76; Charles Francis Adams Jr. to Wells, Apr. 12, Apr. 16, 1872, reel 2, 977–78, 979–80, Wells Papers.
16. Charles Francis Adams, "Diary," Apr. 16, 1872, Adams Papers.
17. David A. Wells to C. F. Adams, Apr. 17, 1872, reel 590, Adams Papers.

Republican movement. Adams betrayed not even a shadow of opposition to the Grant administration. He wrote:

> My Dear Mr. Wells: I have received your letter and will answer it frankly. I do not want the nomination. And could only be induced to consider it by the circumstances under which it might possibly be made. If the call upon me were an unequivocal one, based upon confidence in my character earned in public life, and a belief that I would carry out in practice the principles which I professed, then, indeed, would come a test of my courage; . . . but if I am to be negotiated for, and have assurances given that I am honest, you will be so kind as to draw me out of that crowd. With regard to what I understand to be the declaration of principles which has been made, it would be ridiculous in me to stand haggling over them. With a single exception of ambiguity, I see nothing which any honest Republican or Democrat would not accept. Indeed, I should wonder at anyone who denied them. The difficulty is not in the professions. It lies elsewhere only in the manner in which they are carried into practice.
>
> If I have succeeded in making myself understood, you will perceive that I can give no authority to act or speak for me. . . . I never had a moment's belief that when it came to the point, any one so entirely isolated as I am from all political associations of any kind, could be made acceptable as a candidate for public office; but I am so unlucky as to value that independence more highly than the elevation which is bought by a sacrifice of it. This is not inconsistent with the sense of grateful recognition of the very flattering estimates made of my services in many and high quarters, but I cannot consent to peddle with them for power. If the good people who meet at Cincinnati really believe that they need such an anomalous being as I am (which I do not) they must express it in a manner to convince me of it, or all their labor will be thrown away.[18]

Six days later, on April 24, Adams boarded the *Russia* for Europe and the final Geneva negotiations, thinking that he had avoided the nomination. And the letter did have a chilling effect on his candidacy when Wells permitted it to be published. One fan who had written enthusiastically to Wells, predicting that Adams would "sweep the country," now added a postscript: "Since writing the foregoing I have read Mr. Adam's letter to you which I must frankly say does not strike me as particularly fortunate and attractive. . . ."[19]

The only other candidate acceptable to the reform leaders was Lyman Trumbull, a Connecticut-born Yankee who had moved west to Illinois,

18. Reprinted in *New York Times,* Apr. 25, 1872, p. 5.
19. Edgar T. Wells to Wells, Apr. 25, 1872, reel 2, 998–99, Wells Papers.

won a Senate seat against Abraham Lincoln in 1855, and achieved distinction as the Republican who drafted the antislavery Thirteenth Amendment and the Civil Rights Bill of 1866. By the 1870s, Trumbull recognized that his Republican party had turned into a corrupt patronage machine needlessly prolonging Reconstruction. Trumbull delivered biting indictments of Grant administration abuses but, like Adams, he refused to seek the reform presidential nomination, telling Horace White: "I do not think I ought to be nominated unless there is a decided feeling among those assembled and are outside of rings and bargains, that I would be stronger than anyone else. Unless this is the feeling, I think it would not be wise to present my name at all."[20]

Either frosty New Englander would have satisfied the reform organizers, but their Liberal Republican convention had grown too large for them to control. When idealists enter the political arena, they are tempted to open the doors to those less concerned with ideals like free trade and civil service reform than with office. J. D. Cox had warned Wells that Horace Greeley and Senator Reuben Fenton were organizing a New York delegation to prevent the convention from endorsing free trade. If Greeley succeeded, Cox insisted, the reformers could neither win the fall election nor be the "party of the future." The education of voters in political economy seemed more important to Cox than the mere election of a president in 1872. But other reformers, such as Samuel Bowles, editor of the *Springfield Republican,* pushed accommodating advice—the way to victory came through eliminating the free-trade plank. These wise operators advocated bringing protectionists into the party by emphasizing civil service reform and temporarily dropping the issue of free trade. And so the Bowles opportunists became the managers of the convention, which had begun with a free trade call, and dropped free trade from the platform.[21]

The state delegations that assembled May 1 were largely self-appointed, and while all were required by Edward Atkinson to sign the call, pledging their support of the liberal reforms before entering the convention hall, the delegates were really united only in opposition to President Grant. Disappointed Republican politicians who had been denied their share of the spoils, such as New York Senator Reuben Fenton, were in Cincinnati for the purpose of gaining patronage though the new party. Even in

20. Mark M. Krug, *Lyman Trumbull: Conservative Radical,* 322–25.
21. J. D. Cox to Wells, Apr. 4, 1872, reel 2, 969–73, Wells Papers.

Carl Schurz's own Missouri coalition, eager politicians lusted after office and spoils. Practical politicians were drawn to the convention because overtures between reformers and Democrats promised that the Democratic party would endorse the Cincinnati nominee for the presidency. A combination of reform Republicans and the Democratic party offered realistic hope of defeating President Grant.[22]

Senator Schurz opened the convention in Cincinnati's Exposition Hall with a denunciation of Grantism and a call to restore pure and honest government. Schurz and the independent editors—Horace White, Murat Halstead, Henry Watterson, and Samuel Bowles—believed they were in control and would nominate either Adams or Trumbull. They blocked the ambitious campaign of Supreme Court Justice David Davis, but they failed to stop editor Horace Greeley. They had sought to buy the support of Greeley's *New York Tribune* by compromising their tariff position in the platform, believing the concession would not matter because the economically liberal Adams would be the candidate. Adams did lead on the first ballot, with Trumbull third, but Greeley came in second. And Schurz's jealous Missouri associate, Governor Gratz Brown, who had come in fourth, threw his support behind the candidate most obnoxious to Schurz—Horace Greeley. Six ballots were required but the convention finally went for the candidate regarded as the most "preposterous" by the reform leaders.[23]

Reformers shared little more with Greeley than an antislavery Republican past. He had bitterly opposed most of their reform principles. Greeley had never studied moral philosophy in college. Born in poverty in New Hampshire, Greeley was self-educated, building a belief in protective tariffs from bitter childhood memories of his own mother's handwoven cloth being undersold in the market by British cloth dumped on American merchants. Free trade was unthinkable to Greeley and the only explanation he could imagine for turning Revenue Commissioner David A. Wells against protection was bribery by British gold. Greeley's slander of tariff reformers alone should have disqualified him for the nomination. Greeley should also have been disqualified by his lack of support for civil service reform. As a self-made newspaper publisher who had worked his way up from apprentice without any tests, Greeley had no sympathy with

22. Rhodes, *History of the United States*, 7:38, 42–43; Summers, *Era of Good Stealings*, 214.

23. Logsdon, *Horace White*, 220–33; Trefousse, *Carl Schurz*, 202–5; Ross, *Liberal Republican Movement*, 93–99.

competitive exams. His knowledge had never been subjected to tests and he looked with contempt on all the machinery provided by colleges for testing other people's knowledge. Greeley had been no civil service reformer. On the Liberal Republican issue of returning the South to local self-government and eliminating all Confederate disfranchisement, Greeley had been a late convert. He had even been an advocate of the Radical Republican 1871 Force Bill, which offended the constitutional principles of most Liberal Republicans. Both Democrats and Republican constitutional conservatives thought it dangerous to give President Grant the power to suspend the writ of habeas corpus in time of peace and deny normal constitutional rights. Only in this election year had Greeley decided to abandon his Radical Republican past and make peace with the white South.[24]

Greeley did prove acceptable to Democrats, who cared little about reform, but much about defeating Grant, restoring Democratic patronage, and ending Reconstruction. The Democratic convention in Baltimore gave Greeley a second nomination. Had liberals also been primarily interested in cutting themselves free from Radical Republican Reconstruction, they could easily have joined Democrats in supporting Greeley, but a central group of liberal reformers never endorsed the *Tribune* editor, who E. L. Godkin spoke of as that "conceited, ignorant, half cracked, obstinate old creature."[25]

Liberal reformers—Godkin, David Wells, Edward Atkinson, Henry Adams, William Cullen Bryant, and Jacob D. Cox—never endorsed Greeley. Outraged at the capture of their nomination, they talked of reconvening the convention to nominate a real reform ticket. A Greeley election, they feared, would defeat free-trade and civil service reforms just as surely as Grant's reelection. Greeleyites would make unscrupulous use of patronage to build up a protectionist party. Their best solution would be a "small & select party," established on economic and civil service issues, that would continue their reform movement.[26]

The hope of saving the liberal movement through a splinter party

24. "Party Morality," *Nation* 14 (June 6, 1872): 368; Van Deusen, *Horace Greeley,* 5–14, 328–29.

25. E. L. Godkin to Carl Schurz, May 19, June 28, 1872, in Armstrong, *Gilded Age Letters of E. L. Godkin,* 187, 189–91.

26. J. D. Cox to Wells, May 23, 1872, reel 2, 1018–20; Whitelaw Reid to Samuel Bowles, May 26, 1872, reel 2, 1025, Wells Papers.

never moved beyond discussion. Some of the liberal friends insisted that a splinter movement would only insure the reelection of Grant, while a Greeley victory would destroy the two old bankrupt parties. Even old Senator Lyman Trumbull believed a Greeley victory would "blow up both party organizations" and end the old evils of unprincipled party tyranny. Reform editors Samuel Bowles and Horace White pleaded with David Wells, "Don't you 'go & do it.' What we want to do most," White insisted, "is to destroy and pulverize two old rotten political parties and I think we shall do it." Bowles even tried to explain that they had actually won at the convention. "Cincinnati means political revolution," he told Wells, "the utter extinction and burial of all the issues of the war and a general shaking up of parties, and a new departure."[27]

The old issues of the Civil War had been settled for liberals. None of the David Wells correspondents wrote of Reconstruction and African Americans; they were preoccupied with the troubles created by the war: tariff subsidies, greenbacks, and patronage. Corruption stemming from misguided government policy was their obsession. And since Greeley offered even less promise of change on these issues than Grant, the free-trade Republicans refused to support Greeley.

Political liberals such as Senators Carl Schurz and Lyman Trumbull could persuade themselves to support Greeley. They and Samuel Bowles saw civil service reform and the destruction of parties as more important than free trade. They hoped the mere defeat of Grant could do some good. But economic liberals who saw free trade as the more important reform could not support Greeley. Wells and his free-trade Republicans found it impossible to support the protectionist. They maintained their virtue, holding free-trade meetings and then either voting for Grant or not voting at all.[28]

Liberals took grim satisfaction in Greeley's repudiation by the polls, which prevented their blunder at Cincinnati from continuing to block reform. Greeley's defeat cleared the way for a resumption of liberal reform. Wells and Atkinson were sure they could be the Cobden and Bright of

27. Lyman Trumbull to Wells, May 11, 1872, reel 2, 1005–6; Horace White to Wells, May 17, 1872, reel 1014–15; Samuel Bowles to Wells, May 21, 28, 1872, reel 2, 1016–17, 1029–30, Wells Papers; for the politics of the convention, see Matthew T. Downey, "Horace Greeley and the Politicians: The Liberal Republican Convention in 1872."

28. Ross, *Liberal Republican Movement*, 113; Edward Atkinson to Wells, July 10, 1872, reel 2, 1052–53; J. D. Cox to Wells, Jan. 4, 1873, reel 2, 1150–51, Wells Papers.

the American free-trade movement; they would not abandon their cause just because of the setback of 1872. They laughed at their greenhorn mistakes and plotted anew. And Henry Adams, who had deserted the cause for marriage and an extended foreign honeymoon with Marian Hooper, would be back planning a fresh independent effort.

6

Dismay with Democracy

Liberal reformers celebrated the one hundredth anniversary of Adam Smith's *Wealth of Nations* with a banquet at Delmonico's in New York City in 1876. There David A. Wells led after-dinner cheers for the book that had created their liberalism by shifting conventional wisdom away from a Hobbesian belief in war and exploitation as the natural condition, to a liberal belief that freedom and prosperity resulted from governments standing back and permitting individuals to practice the golden rule in the markets.[1] Yet that cheer and optimism characteristic of liberals, from Adam Smith through Richard Cobden, Francis Wayland, and John Stuart Mill, must have been a bit forced because of recent rude shocks that went unmentioned in the centennial celebration at Delmonico's. Liberals were dismayed that Americans ignored Adam Smith's teachings and pursued self-interest through government policy, seeking tariffs, inflation, and easy money rather than public virtue and the general good.

The depression decade of the 1870s had provided ample evidence for questioning liberal optimism, but some disappointment may have been the inevitable consequence of aging on the liberal reformers. Now in their forties, E. L. Godkin, Horace White, and Charles Eliot Norton had lost that optimism of the young that they would never be old, never be sick, and never be defeated. These three had now lost a spouse and a child to the ill health that was endemic to city life before the discovery of germs and the sanitation revolution. In their personal tragedy they were without

1. *New York Times,* Dec. 13, 1876, 5; the dinner had been proposed to promote "Free Trade, Hard Money, and Civil Service Reform," R. R. Bowker to David A. Wells, Jan. 11, 1876, reel 4, 2055, Wells Papers; for the liberal interpretation of capitalism, see Haskell, "Capitalism and the Origins of Humanitarian Sensibility," or John Stuart Mill's reference to the golden rule of Jesus as a perfect expression of utilitarian morality, Robson, *Collected Works of John Stuart Mill,* 10:218.

the comfort of religion, for, like most Mugwumps, they had moved from the age of faith to the age of science.[2] They had exchanged their belief in the Christian myths and the divine hand for a faith that educated citizens would act in accordance with scientific laws and the personal ethic of Christian benevolence.

The laws for liberal reformers were found in social science and taught by the American Association for the Study of Social Science. These laws were products of the assumption that study of human experience provided the best guide for regulating the behavior of people. Social scientists believed human experience had been a laboratory of experimentation, providing answers to public questions. Study of the past gave Mugwumps their economic and government policies. Godkin explained, "History and political economy and jurisprudence are neither more nor less than a catalogue of the results of experiments in living made by many generations of men, which the art of writing has preserved for our benefit. . . ."[3] Liberal reformers used history with surprising thoroughness and insight, supporting their moral positions with data they regarded as scientific.

The trouble for liberal independents was that the majority of politicians refused to share their faith in the lessons of the past. America, according to popular thought, lived free from the troubles and rules of the old world. Wisdom from the past had no power in a new land. Repudiation of historical experience became a dominant theme in the depression of the seventies. When investment banker Jay Cooke failed in September 1873, touching off a financial panic and a grinding economic depression persisting for five years, politicians abandoned the lessons of human experience and responded to voter demands for a quick fix on economic troubles. When Congress convened after the collapse of Cooke and Company, a five-month debate on an inflation bill followed.[4]

Congressmen assembling in December 1873 were eager to provide a political solution for the country's financial difficulties. Convinced that a scarcity of money had deflated the booming business of the nation, politicians agreed that businessmen and farmers needed more money.

2. For pessimism, see Logsdon, *Horace White*, 266–69, 329–30; Vanderbilt, *Charles Eliot Norton*, 114–15; Armstrong, *E. L. Godkin: A Biography*, 137–38.
3. Haskell, *Emergence of Professional Social Science*, 91–105; E. L. Godkin, "The Proper Study of Mankind," *Nation* 17 (July 3, 1873): 5.
4. To see the debate through a Mugwump filter, read Charles Francis Adams Jr., "The Currency Debate of 1873–74," *North American Review* 119 (July 1874): 111–65; for scholarly neutrality, see Unger, *Greenback Era*, 213–48.

In urging an expansion of the currency, congressmen violated one of the most established tenets of political economy. Even moderate expansionists such as Senator Oliver P. Morton objected to letting recessions "run their course" like measles or smallpox. They wanted to doctor the economy with a dose of government paper, and the dosage need only be small: the forty-four million greenbacks that Secretary McCulloch had retired in 1866. "It does not take much to start the wheels," Senator Morton said, "but when the wheels of trade are started their revolution becomes faster and faster." The economy would be made to move again, just like an old dry pump into which the farmer could "pour a quart of water in the top" and then pump all day.[5]

Independents took the "absurdities and atrocities" of this pump-priming argument as evidence of appalling ignorance. All students knew monetary expansion could only reignite the cycle of inflationary boom and economic bust that had created the depression. Relief through inflation would be no relief at all. And still congressmen got up and said, "I want to see speculation . . . to see this country grow, flourish, and develop." From the debates, it appeared to Charles Francis Adams Jr. that a majority of the statesmen were "utterly uninformed as to the simplest axioms of political economy."[6]

In the eyes of the independents, congressmen were not only ignorant but hypocritical and perhaps even swindlers. Politicians claimed no respect for the "wealth and intelligence" of the country but openly favored the "unfortunate debtor class." They described the greenback issue as a question of whether the laborer should "walk more erect, or the capitalist more proudly strut." Contemptuous of the bankers and men of wealth, politicians declared: "These men produce nothing, add nothing to wealth; they toil not, neither do they spin. . . . They are the drones in the hive of industry . . . they are the buzzards who batten and fatten on the corruption of the body politic." E. L. Godkin exploded with contempt for the hypocritical "poor debtor" argument. Poor men rarely had much debt because no one would trust them with much money. The really great debtors were the rich who borrowed from banks and insurance companies. "They are great merchants, or manufacturers, or brokers, or contractors, or railroad-builders," Godkin said. "In fact, in so far as the debtors can be called a class, they form a very small class, and a class of

5. *Congressional Record,* 43d Cong., 1st sess., 301.
6. Adams, "Currency Debate of 1873–74," 130.

enormous power, over whom it is ludicrous for the government to exercise a fatherly care."[7]

While they opposed legislative inflationists—Morton, Logan, Ferry, and Butler—independents applauded Carl Schurz, John Sherman, and Allen Thurman for their verbal duels with the enemies of sound money. Schurz was the pride of the liberals, for he "unhesitatingly flung himself into the struggle, in obedience to his convictions, and boldly risked his political future on a faith in his principles." Had Schurz's colleagues only listened, they would have learned traditional economic wisdom, lessons taken by Schurz from the texts of Amasa Walker's *Science of Wealth* and John Stuart Mill's *Principles of Political Economy*. From his reading of classical economists, Schurz understood that governments were incapable of maintaining the value of paper money.[8]

But Congress dismissed Schurz as a German immigrant who took his learning from books and so knew nothing of America or of practical affairs. Fellow Senators rejected the lessons of human experience explained by classical economists. Morton, for example, declared, "I put aside all these old theories . . . doctrines drawn from the experience of old and small countries are not adapted to a country like ours, that is growing and developing and is now but in its youth." Morton preferred to draw his own conclusions about the needs of America, and to "let theory go to the dogs."[9]

All of this discouraged independents, who believed that the world should listen to scholars such as Adam Smith and the Manchester economists. But in the Senate these acknowledged authorities found little support. "Are we to be whistled down the wind and answered by theories from John Stuart Mill or from Bastiat?" demanded Senator Morton. And in the House, William D. Kelley expressed his conviction that *a priori* ideas derived from the old classical teachers were the most dangerous knowledge a legislator could possess. Representative Hezekiah Bundy of Ohio was glad he had not read political economy. "If I had," he said, "I might have adopted their heresies."[10]

Because demagogues sneered in "ignorance" at the financial principles

7. E. L. Godkin, "The Debtor Class," *Nation* 18 (Apr. 23, 1874): 262; Adams, "The Currency Debate of 1873–74," 134–41.

8. *Congressional Record*, 43d Cong., 1st sess., Jan. 14, 1974, 640–46.

9. Ibid., Jan. 15, 669.

10. "Theory and Practice," *Harper's Weekly* 18 (Mar. 14, 1874): 122; Adams, "Currency Debate of 1873–74," 162–63; *Congressional Record*, 43d Cong., 1st sess., Jan. 27, 1727–30.

that had been accepted by the "most careful and thoughtful students," reformers were convinced that Congress was at odds with the intelligence of the country. "Don't join the black sheep," Edward Atkinson warned Iowa Senator William Boyd Allison. "Truth is truth and will prevail." To expand the currency would be "to play fast and loose with all values!"[11]

But Congress ignored reformer advice. In April 1874, it voted to expand the currency by $18 million in greenbacks and $46 million in National Bank notes. Politicians regarded the bill as a compromise with inflationists; the currency expansion was too small to create any real inflation. But independents sounded the alarm because any paper currency created by Congress was wrong and because this inflation bill, they feared, was only the opening wedge. This bill, it was said, would launch the country upon another era of inflation like that of the French assignats or the Continental currency. Now that the dike of honesty had been broken, further issues of paper money would follow, until universal ruin and bankruptcy fell upon the land.[12]

When reformers lost influence with Congress, they united with bankers and merchants. Protest meetings in Boston and New York sought a presidential check against the currency expansion bill, and Edward Atkinson spent twenty-five dollars telegraphing western business associates in Milwaukee, St. Louis, Chicago, and Cincinnati, urging them to rain protests in on Grant. These western telegrams, signed by men of reputation, apparently convinced Grant that public opinion opposed the bill. His surprise veto won reformer applause; the national honor had been saved but not the reputation of Congress. As Charles Francis Adams Jr. said, educated people had been shocked that such "vile sophistries" had been spoken outside a "lunatic asylum" in the latter half of the nineteenth century.[13]

The only solution for misguided politicians in a democracy had to be public education. Reformers must teach the public to condemn inflationary legislation. Especially in the West, it seemed to E. L. Godkin and the reformers, average voters lacked the most elementary principles of political economy. To educate millions of voters on the money question,

11. Edward Atkinson to William B. Allison, Mar. 21, 1874; Atkinson to Allison, Apr. 12, 1874, William B. Allison Papers, Historical Department of Iowa, Des Moines, Iowa.
12. E. L. Godkin, "The Inflation Vote," *Nation* 18 (Apr. 2, 1874): 214; "The Era of Assignats," *Harper's Weekly* 18 (Apr. 11, 1874): 310.
13. Adams, "Currency Debate of 1873–74," 125.

popular lectures and the distribution of books and pamphlets were the only way.[14]

So Carl Schurz told western audiences that a government-regulated currency was like a bad tooth. "However severely the decayed grinder may pain you," he said, "you are apt to dread the moment when the tooth is drawn." But one would be a fool to run around with a toothache for fear of the dentist. Just as pulling the tooth put an end to a toothache, so contraction of the greenbacks would remedy the financial malady. "Our decayed tooth has to come out some time; the sooner it is out the better," Schurz said. "You give a shriek perhaps when the tooth comes, but feel so much the more comfortable afterwards, and then you are sorry that you did not submit to the operation sooner." With such homespun analogies, Schurz sought to persuade the West to abandon greenback currency, which gave government "a dangerous and despotic power" over the private fortunes of the citizenry.[15]

As his contribution to the financial education of the American public, William Graham Sumner, a Yale professor and cousin of E. L. Godkin's wife, rushed to the press with a treatise called *The History of American Currency* (1874). The book sought to establish fundamental doctrines by "going back to history." Sumner found that paper money, from colonial days to the present, had always been disastrous, morally and economically. Inflated currency caused a deterioration of public morals and a contempt for patient industry. Financially it led to erratic heats and chills, ending in ruin and repudiation.

Sumner found all the answers in English monetary history. At the end of his book, he appended the *Bullion Report,* a document that had been the "intellectual cause" for the English decision to resume specie payments in 1819. Since the *Bullion Report,* Sumner said, nothing new had been discovered about the working of paper money; the established doctrines remained undisputed. The tenets had been verified by experience and were the established basis of finance. Like Newton's theory of gravity, the doctrines had passed the stage where the scientific financier was bound to discuss them.[16]

14. "Political Economy in the West," *New York Times,* Jan. 23, 1874, p. 4; E. L. Godkin, "Popular Protection against Financial Quackery," *Nation* 21 (Sept. 30, 1875): 209.

15. "Speech of Carl Schurz," *St. Louis Democrat,* Sept. 25, 1874, Schurz Scrapbooks, Library of Congress.

16. William Graham Sumner, *A History of American Currency* (New York: Henry Holt, 1874), 248–50.

The history of paper currency revealed the evil consequences of inflation and national bankruptcy. Sumner found nations unable to fix limits that would prevent further issuance of paper money; such limits were never respected. "A man might as well jump off a precipice intending to stop half way down" as to attempt to expand the currency with irredeemable money and then stop at a fixed limit. History proved that government currency led to inflation and repudiation. Only Great Britain had ever safely returned from a paper currency to a gold standard.[17]

To undercut belief in greenbacks, independents insisted that paper currency was not money. Simon Newcomb, a Harvard astronomer, pursued this line of argument in "The ABC of Finance: or, the Money Question Familiarly Explained to Every-Day People, in Nine Short and Easy Lessons." Newcomb's lessons were simple and readable. It might seem incredible that any economist would deny that government gives fiat money its value, yet Newcomb confidently asserted that this idea was "as pure a superstition" as the old notion that a witch could torture a victim by conjuring up a wax image and jabbing it with pins. Newcomb, like all classical economists, defined money so narrowly that only a commodity with intrinsic value, such as gold or silver, could fit the definition. Newcomb explained that the greenback had value only because the holders expected them to be redeemed within a generation. The government had promised to redeem the notes with gold, and the people believed it would.[18]

As to why so few congressmen were qualified to legislate on the money question, Newcomb attributed their weakness to lack of education. Most politicians, he said, simply had not mastered the intricacies of the problem. Newcomb assured his readers, however, that there were capable men outside of Congress who were authorities. He suggested that if a poll were taken among "the political economists, the close students, the bankers, the professors, and the historians," the vote for fiat money would be "astonishingly small." Experts knew best, and Americans should adopt their opinions.

Once Americans suffered enough pain from paper money, David A. Wells told readers of the *New York Herald*, they would endorse his "cremation theory" of resumption. If the Treasury built a bonfire once a week and burned $500,000 in greenbacks, $26 million a year, the gradual

---

17. Ibid., 215.
18. Simon Newcomb, "The ABC of Finance," *Harper's Weekly* vol. 19 (Dec. 18, 1875): 1018; (Dec. 25, 1875): 1042; vol. 20 (Jan. 1, 1876): 10; (Jan. 8, 1876): 31; Simon Newcomb, *The Reminiscences of an Astronomer* (Boston: Houghton Mifflin, 1903), 400.

contraction would appreciate greenbacks to par with gold within four years. And as his contribution to popular education, Wells wrote a novel, *Robinson Crusoe's Money* (1876), to expose all the historical fallacies of money and credit.[19]

While reformers were conducting public education classes in the evils of greenbacks, another inflationary panacea slipped up on them. Silver became a popular means of raising prices after its market price began to fall in 1872. Silver bullion grew cheaper as increased silver production flooded the market. As the market price declined, the gold value of the silver dollar fell from $1.02 in 1872 to $0.85 by 1876. Once silver was cheap, money expansionists turned from greenbacks to silver, arguing that expanding the money supply with silver would revive the nation from the nadir of economic depression.[20]

When John Percival Jones, Senator from the silver-mining state of Nevada, asked for monetary expansion to restore national prosperity, Congress gave him a Monetary Commission to pack with silver-mining men, then published a Senate report on his bold manifesto for an expansion of the currency. The Monetary Commission assumed that government ought to increase the money supply to stop the general price decline. Falling prices had frightened industrialists into shutting down their furnaces to avert major losses, the Commission said. As declining prices made money more valuable, capitalists hoarded their gold and refused to lend. This downward spiral, which bankrupted enterprising borrowers and threw laborers into unemployment, would continue, the Commission insisted, until the remonetization of silver brought price increases, stopped hoarding, and caused money to again flow through the arteries of the nation.[21]

Permitting politicians to manipulate prices along with the money supply had always been unacceptable to liberal economists. The markets, not governments, could be trusted to make these decisions. To be sure, silver had an intrinsic value, like gold, but the essential question, according to the Senate minority report, written by Professor Francis Bowen of Harvard, asked whether fluctuations in the value of the metal rendered

19. *New York Herald,* Feb. 13, 1875, p. 5; David A. Wells, *Robinson Crusoe's Money* (New York: Harper, 1876).

20. Unger, *Greenback Era,* 328–49.

21. Senate, *Report of the Monetary Commission,* 44th Cong., 2d sess., 1877, S. Rept. 703, 53–60; for the Jones story, see Allen Weinstein, *Prelude to Populism: Origins of the Silver Issue, 1867–1878,* 53–81, 244–49.

it unacceptable as money. Since silver had declined sharply in value and the industrial nations of Europe had rejected it as money, Bowen asserted that Congress could never keep the value of the silver dollar equal to that of gold.[22]

Liberal reformers actually suffered the defection of a few believers in these silver debates. To be sure, in an ideal world the value of money should not change because when it did, some groups gained and others lost. To avoid such a redistribution of wealth, Professor Francis A. Walker of Yale suggested an international silver agreement. Bimetallism, as it was called, would be more complex and less convenient than the single gold standard, but Walker thought uniting inflationary silver with deflationary gold would restore a horizonal price trend, creating a healthier and more vigorous economy.[23]

Walker became a heretic in reform circles. Gold had become the standard for Europe while silver had become the hope of former greenback inflationists, so liberals were virtually all for gold. No freedom for deviate theory was tolerated by the reform press in the social crisis of the seventies when striking railway workers were fighting federal troops in the streets of eastern cities in the summer of 1877. Arson, murder, and looting were terrifying outrages in this first national railway strike. And the frightened *Nation* editors began to use the word "communist" for demonstrations of the unemployed carrying red flags as well as for anarchistic attacks in Russia and the earlier seizure of Paris by communards. Class war threatened to tear society apart and, exemplifying Mugwump fear, Harvard's President Charles Eliot promoted a rifle club and armed drilling among the college students. "He thinks," a Cambridge Mugwump explained, "the time may likely soon come when they will need to know the use of arms,—not to defend the college, but for service in some one or other of the cities."[24]

The violence of strike rhetoric spilled over into the silver debates. Actually, the division was based more on sectional differences than on class distinctions. By 1877, western and southern farmers were supporting silver with an enthusiasm they had never given paper money. Western

22. *Report of the Monetary Commission,* 151–60.

23. Francis A. Walker, *Money* (New York: Holt, 1878), 78–94; Walker, "The Monetary Conferences of 1867 and 1878, and the Future of Silver," *Princeton Review* 3 (Jan. 1879): 28–54; Weinstein, *Prelude to Populism,* 129–37, gives an overview of early silver confusion among reformers.

24. Norton to J. R. Lowell, May 19, 1878, in Norton and Howe, *Letters of Charles Eliot Norton,* 2:81.

businessmen in the Cincinnati and St. Paul Chambers of Commerce endorsed remonetization, and so did merchants in Chicago, Toledo, and St. Louis. Support among merchants was so strong that a majority of the National Board of Trade voted to ask Congress to coin $50 million of the metal. The *American Manufacturer*, western industrialists, real estate brokers, and even some western bankers turned towards silver.[25]

Backed by widespread public support, western and southern congressmen flocked to Washington in the fall of 1877, eager to expand the currency. The House majority suspended debate and passed Richard P. Bland's free-coinage bill by a vote of 163 to 34. Gold-standard men were overwhelmed. The Senate offered little resistance to Bland's bill. Indiana Senator Daniel W. Vorhees even warned that labor violence, like the alarming railway strikes, might be the price of refusal to adopt free silver. With no sympathy for liberal economics, Vorhees sought a return to the inflationary climate of the sixties. Those had been prosperous times, he said, when "good wages and good prices stimulated every laboring-man's muscle, every businessman's brain, and every power of machinery into the most productive activity." This view of inflation was precisely what reformers sought to resist. To their thinking, the inflationary years of the sixties instead had been a time when moral values were overturned, the lessons of economics ignored, and the advantage given to speculators rather than the thrifty and industrious.[26]

Reformers had few allies in resistance to the silver expansionists. Treasury Secretary John Sherman compromised along with other politicians to make a deal for recoinage. Even eastern banking circles were willing to concede that some type of silver legislation was inevitable. And the Senate did amend the silver bill, substituting for the free-coinage clause a smaller monthly purchase of $2 million to $4 million of silver bullion. For politicians, this amendment enabled the Bland-Allison Act to pass the Senate with a two-thirds majority on February 15, 1878.[27]

Reformers were unwilling to accept Bland-Allison. As the Yale professor William Graham Sumner wrote, "to regulate the value of money is to fix

25. Unger, *Greenback Era*, 333–35; one Mugwump in Congress, J. D. Cox, voted for silver, first, as a strategy to block paper inflation, and second, because he agreed with Walker's *Money* that "throwing away half the coin of the world will double the value of the other half," doubling debts and creating revolution. See Cox to Wells, Feb. 28, 1878, reel 5, 3019–21, Wells Papers.

26. "Representative Government," *Harper's Weekly* 22 (Feb. 16, 1878): 126.

27. John Sherman, *Recollections of Forty Years* (New York: Werner, 1895), 2:623.

prices, and Congress has never tried that since it existed." Even if moving to a single gold standard had produced "temporary disorder, loss, and suffering," this was no justification for monetary manipulation. Men must adjust to the unavoidable changes that accompany the natural evolution of society. "The economic development of human society must go on its way and work out its results," Sumner wrote, "and the human race must make the best of them." When men refused to accommodate themselves to change, they disrupted the natural course of development.[28]

Because the silver bill was a governmental attempt to fix the value of money, reformers demanded that the bill be killed, and President Rutherford B. Hayes vetoed the legislation with the assertion that national honor must be maintained. The nation had a "sacred" obligation to preserve contracts, and any legislation to legalize depreciated silver coin would do irreparable damage to public faith. Hayes's action redeemed him in the eyes of reformers but carried no weight in Congress. On February 28, 1878, without discussion, Congress repassed the Bland-Allison Act over the presidential veto.[29]

Politicians understood Bland-Allison as the compromise with soft-money interests, the necessary concession required before the nation could be permitted to return to the gold standard. Four years before, a divided Republican Congress had adopted the pretense of a currency policy, promising to resume specie payments in five years, on January 1, 1879. The Resumption Act had been only a political appearance of action, an empty Republican declaration, but because the nation began running a favorable trade balance with the rest of the world in 1878, paper money grew toward par value. On December 17, 1878, the greenbacks could be exchanged evenly for gold dollars; the following day the Gold Room on Wall Street closed because greenbacks no longer had a speculative value; and on January 2, 1879, the U.S. Treasury began to redeem greenbacks with gold dollars.

Reformers might justly claim much of the credit for a return to the gold standard. During the seventeen years of irredeemable greenbacks, the reform press had stood firm in support of a gold standard and the lessons of history, while politicians, businessmen, and farmers had equivocated. E. L. Godkin of the *Nation* took credit with the newspapers for being the "rational, reflective, remembering element in society" that

28. William Graham Sumner, "Bimetallism," *Princeton Review* 4 (Nov. 1879): 546–78.
29. "Paying the Piper," *Harper's Weekly* 22 (Mar. 9, 1878): 186.

saved American civilization from some of the worst monetary "folly and ignorance."[30]

Godkin shared credit for resumption with Christian ministers who had treated financial heresies as forms of sin—cheating. While he preferred to oppose greenbacks with the evidence of history, New York City financiers had concluded that the moral argument was the wisest argument to use against the inflationists. Godkin found it depressing that financiers did not believe financial questions could be successfully explained in a democracy. And he had feared that the Christian religion had lost power with the masses who were becoming more skeptical, looking on Christianity as a "cunningly devised fable intended to reconcile the poor and unhappy to their lot. . . ." But when resumption happened, Godkin must have concluded that faith and religion had persisted, for he thanked the ministers as well as the newspaper editors for restoring the gold standard.[31]

Yet liberal reformers were not pleased with the political compromise that brought a return to the gold standard. Redeemed greenbacks were to be returned to circulation, leaving $346 million greenbacks in the money supply. Every student of political economy knew banks and not governments should supply the redeemable paper currency. The mere existence of government paper would be temptation for all inflationists to lobby for expansion of the greenback supply.[32]

Greenbacks were also jeopardized by the Bland-Allison Act, which required the annual addition of $24 million of silver dollars to the currency. With greenbacks redeemable in either gold or silver, the gold reserve might become depleted while the silver reserve piled up in the treasury. Gresham's law of political economy predicted that every cheap silver dollar acquired by the treasury would crowd out a gold dollar. It followed that the treasury would gain a larger and larger stock of silver from its monthly purchases, while the gold dollars were withdrawn. When the gold reserve declined below a safety margin, holders of greenbacks would panic at the possibility of silver payments and rush in to exchange their notes for the remaining gold.[33]

30. E. L. Godkin, "Resumption," *Nation* 27 (Dec. 26, 1878): 294.
31. Ibid.; E. L. Godkin, "Sumner's History of American Currency," *Nation* 18 (Apr. 23, 1874): 267; E. L. Godkin, "Woolsey's Political Science," *Nation* 26 (May 9, 1878): 310.
32. Horace White, "After Specie Resumption—What?" *International Review* 5 (Oct. 1878): 845.
33. Ibid., 834.

If the treasury were forced to suspend gold payments and to redeem greenbacks in silver, the paper currency would depreciate 18 percent to the bullion value of a silver dollar. For reformers, passage of the Bland-Allison Act was analogous to placing a "cage of wild beasts" among helpless people. Most people would be unaware of the ferocity of the animals. Only alert reformers could see that the bars of the cage were almost gnawed through; and they lived in fear of what would happen "if the silver dollars got out."[34]

No breakdown of gold payments ever occurred, so liberal fears are most useful as evidence of the extreme reformer pessimism about the American political system. The deepest trough of the seventies depression, 1878, was the year some Mugwumps began to declare democracy a failure. Henry Adams began his savage satire *Democracy* that year. Francis Parkman published his "The Failure of Universal Suffrage" in the *North American Review,* declaring that "flinging the suffrage to the mob" had been disastrous in the cities and in the American South. The Irish and the African American voters had used politics for plunder. The duty of old abolitionists, and taxpayers, according to Parkman, was to take back the cities. And at the *Nation,* E. L. Godkin and Horace White were writing about going to the barricades and making a stand against Bland and the "communists" of the National Labor-Greenback party, whose "wild and incomprehensible" platform called for inflation and a graduated income tax. The *Nation* accused silver agitators of poisoning the minds of workers with class hatred and "the dregs of European communism." E. L. Godkin insisted that reformers must make it clear that "communists will be killed" if they attempted to carry out their theories.[35]

Hard times seriously damaged liberal optimism. When distressed individuals successfully legislated their selfish interests in politics, Mugwumps feared Americans would never be capable of putting public interest before private desires. In the economic depression of the 1870s, and again in the depression of the 1890s, great majorities turned away from the free market to demand special legislation. Mugwumps were, to be sure, deeply disappointed. Experience with the practice of democracy left their opinion

---

34. J. Laurence Laughlin, "The Silver Danger," *Atlantic Monthly* 53 (May 1884): 677.

35. Ernest Samuels, introduction to Henry Adams, *Democracy* and *Esther* (Garden City: Doubleday, 1961), xii; Francis Parkman, "The Failure of Universal Suffrage," *North American Review* 127 (July 1878): 1–20; Horace White, "Communism and Protection at the Capital," *Nation* 26 (Feb. 28, 1878): 146–47; E. L. Godkin, "The Communistic Movement," *Nation* 26 (May 9, 1878): 302; E. L. Godkin, "The Sources of Communism," *Nation* 26 (May 16, 1878): 318.

of voters shot through with ambivalence. But the pessimism of their despair in the depth of a depression would not accurately characterize the group. They never really gave up in despair, except for the Adams brothers and Godkin, who finally abandoned hope in the 1890s. For most Mugwumps, their sense of duty and their essential optimism always brought them back to doing their duty as public moralists in a democracy.

7

Independents Achieve Mugwump Victory

The name *Mugwump* won a permanent place in history because political independents were proud of their success in the presidential election of 1884. This derisive epithet, flung by Republican regulars, would never have been adopted if independents had lost that political contest. To be sure, the scholarly independents knew the origin of *mugwump* to have been an Algonquian word for "great leader" or "chief," but they did not commonly call themselves Mugwumps until they had defeated James G. Blaine's presidential ambitions. They then took up the new name with pride, saluting the fellow Mugwump with a joy not unlike a later generation's high five. Pride of performance let independents adopt the new name.

The Mugwump victory owed much to the tradition of public morality that had been maintained in families such as the Adams family. The founding father, President John Adams, had done the right thing by avoiding war with France rather than winning reelection as a war president in 1800, and his sense of public virtue persisted through four generations of Adamses. Charles Francis Adams Senior, of the third generation, retained all the Christian republican virtue of his grandfather; he may have lacked the temper and ambition of the founder but not the puritanical conscience condemning the pursuit of material ends at the expense of community good. On his return from Europe in 1873, the short, stout Adams naturally would have liked recognition by an appointment to President Grant's cabinet, but he refused to seek any office, because traditional republican virtue did not permit self-promotion and because he really preferred to be out of public life. Appalled by the corruption of the Grant administration and the disappearance of "moral principle" from the Republican party,

Adams feared that republican government would fail in America. The pessimistic Adams predicted no hope of revival in moral principle, and he saw himself as too old—he was seventy years of age in 1876—to lead a moral reconstruction. "I have no faith in any reform during my time," he told his diary, and he thereby permitted himself to leave reform to "the next generation."[1]

The fourth generation of Adams—Henry and Charles Francis Jr.—retained the family concern with republican virtue but not its religious dimension. They grew beyond the Christian faith of their father, who had continued the puritan practice of taking notes on the minister's sermon and reading religious books on Sunday. The elder Adams lamented that he had not given better religious instruction to his children. "God forgive me for this oversight," Charles Francis wrote in 1873. "My children are moral and upright but they are not religious."[2]

The shift from religious to secular virtue in the fourth generation of the family did not change the Adams position on public service. Values statements of Henry Adams could sound much like those of his father. Henry asserted that "no man should be in politics unless he would honestly rather not be there. Public service should be . . . a disagreeable necessity." But Henry reflected a more secular perspective in doubting that moral virtue could resist the destructive nature of politics. Henry cautioned his former student Henry Cabot Lodge:

> politics deteriorate the moral tone of everyone who mixes in them. The deterioration is far more marked than in any other occupation I know except the turf, stock-jobbing, and gambling.
>
> I have never known a young man go into politics who was not the worse for it. . . . They all try to be honest, and then are tripped up by the dishonest; or they try to be dishonest (i.e. practical politicians) and degrade their own natures. In the first case they become disappointed and bitter; in the other they lose self-respect.[3]

Adams reflected bedrock Mugwump moral philosophy: pursuing political office killed character, the moral quality that most distinguished

1. Charles Francis Adams, "Diary," Feb. 2, Mar. 7, May 8, 1873, Aug. 7, Sept. 8, 1876, reel 85, Adams Papers; see also Joseph J. Ellis, *Passionate Sage: The Character and Legacy of John Adams* (New York: W. W. Norton, 1993); and Martin B. Duberman, *Charles Francis Adams* (Boston: Houghton Mifflin, 1960).

2. Charles Francis Adams, "Diary," Dec. 14, 1873, reel 85, Adams Papers.

3. Adams to Henry Cabot Lodge, Nov. 15, 1881, in Levenson et al., *Letters of Henry Adams,* 2:444.

the best men. If avoidance of self-interest distinguished Victorian men, then resisting the temptations of the lower self ought to be the guiding light of educated young men. So the path to preserving moral principle should be altruistic public reform and not the search for elected office. Adams offered Mugwump wisdom that character could be best preserved by serving as a public moralist and not as a politician.

Today, Henry Adams has the reputation of a pessimistic historian, but in the 1870s, he was a young reform activist who hoped to change the system. His early activism in the Liberal Republican movement of 1872 had been diverted by engagement and marriage to Marian Hooper, but three years later Henry boldly launched another independent party, telling an English friend: "I am engaged single-handed in the slight task of organizing a new party to contest the next Presidential election in '76. As yet I have only three allies; a broken down German politician; a newspaper correspondent, and a youth of twenty who is to do all the work."[4]

Henry's allies were actually more numerous than Carl Schurz, Sam Bowles of the *Springfield Republican,* and Henry Cabot Lodge, a new Harvard Ph.D. in history. Two Adams brothers, Charles Francis Jr. and Brooks, were in the reform party, along with Moorfield Storey and a few other young Bostonians determined to force one of the major parties to accept Henry's father as their presidential candidate. The Boston reformers joined New York independents for a dinner to honor retiring Senator Carl Schurz at Delmonico's, April 27, and a conference to rally independents around a reform presidential candidate. The initial plan of an Adams candidacy collapsed when the dour older Adams attracted insufficient support. The independents then became a Bristow club, supporting Secretary of the Treasury Benjamin H. Bristow because he had stopped the whiskey ring frauds in his department. This professional politician never fully identified with the reformers, yet he could not win the Republican presidential nomination in 1876. The reformers were too weak to name the Republican candidate but powerful enough for their delegates, led by Carl Schurz and George W. Curtis, to deny any spoilsman the nomination. When the convention chose the dark-horse Governor Rutherford B. Hayes of Ohio, independents felt empowered that their veto had blocked Morton, Conkling, and Blaine.[5]

4. Adams to Charles Milnes Gaskell, Feb. 15, 1875, in Levenson et al., *Letters of Henry Adams,* 2:217.

5. Adams to Carl Schurz, Apr. 12, 1875; Adams to David A. Wells, Apr. 20, 1875, Adams to Gaskell, Feb. 9, 1876, June 14, 1876, in Levenson et al., *Letters of Henry Adams,* 2:222, 223, 247, 276; John A. Garraty, *Henry Cabot Lodge: A Biography,* 40–46.

A second attractive choice for reformers, Samuel J. Tilden, won the 1876 Democratic nomination. The New York governor, who had destroyed the corrupt Tweed Ring, divided independents between two promising presidential candidates. Schurz deserted to Hayes, without even conferring with his fellow independents, because the Republican was sound on the reform issues and would give him a cabinet position. The Adamses thought Hayes a "third-rate" leader too weak to force his Republican party to give up patronage and corruption. Hayes possessed good character, but his election could not reform his party, which had held power for fifteen years and failed to provide leadership of the tariff, currency, and civil service reform. Only the discipline of defeat might force Republicans to recognize the necessity of reform. Tilden offered promise of immediate results; as a hard-money Democrat, he could force a return to the gold standard, and as a free-trade Democrat, he could compel tariff reductions. Tilden had already used his influence to have the Democratic party of Massachusetts unanimously nominate Charles Francis Adams Sr. as their candidate for governor. The elder Adams did not wish to be elected, but he appreciated the honor so much that he repressed his dour personality and avoided "coldness" and "hesitation." The flattery from Tilden surely helped the Adams family and Henry Cabot Lodge vote Democratic for Tilden in 1876.[6]

The Adamses and Lodge were outraged when Republicans stole the presidential election of 1876, even though Tilden had won a 250,000 popular-vote majority and surely an electoral majority. By counting Hayes the winner of all electoral votes in contested states, Republicans refused to turn the presidency over to a Democrat. Charles Francis Adams Sr. understood the election as evidence that the rottenness of the Republican organization could even cancel the will of the voters.[7]

In the aftermath of the contested election of 1876, Henry Adams completed his savage satire *Democracy* (1880), in which his pompous, corrupt Senator Silas P. Ratcliffe, a fictional James G. Blaine, had stolen an election to "save this country from disunion," sold his Senate vote for money—which should have sent him to prison—and ridiculed all possibility of reform. Senator Ratcliffe was a "moral lunatic" who could

---

6. Charles Francis Adams, "Diary," Sept. 6, 1876; Henry Adams and Charles Francis Adams Jr., "The 'Independents' in the Canvass," *North American Review* 122 (Oct. 1876): 426–65; Adams to David A. Wells, *Letters of Henry Adams*, 2:282; Fuess, *Carl Schurz*, 226.

7. Charles Francis Adams, "Diary," Feb. 17, 1877, reel 87, Adams Papers.

not see the difference between "a lie and the truth" and who "talked about virtue and vice as a man who is colorblind talks about red and green."[8]

Tough twentieth-century writers might ridicule Adams for sitting on the sidelines and writing poor fiction rather than entering politics and making a real contribution, but public moralists have always been in shorter supply than politicians. And young Henry Adams could not be accurately described as a spectator; he used his pen as a tool to persuade educated Americans that Republican leaders lacked moral principle. He also used his pen as an organizing tool to bring independents into an influential bloc for the presidential selections of 1872 and 1876. Among the college-educated in New York and Boston, moral reform clubs, civil service groups, free trade leagues, and good government clubs were asserting the interest of public morality in politics. "Young Scratchers" in New York eliminated unacceptable Republican candidates from their printed ballots. Young independents no longer needed Adams's leadership, and he, forty years old in 1878, began to speak of himself as an old man who would leave the activism to youngsters.[9]

In New York City the thirty-year-old R. R. Bowker seized the reins for independents in the 1879 "Young Scratcher" campaign. The Massachusetts-born and New York–educated dynamo of energy had graduated from college a decade before, with the moral philosophy teachings that led him to join older independents in the American Free Trade League, meeting, organizing, and resolution-drafting, promoting freedom from government regulation. Bowker created new groups—Free Trade Alliance and Free Trade Club—to attract younger reformers. And he harassed older independents for being too timid to take on patronage bosses. Bowker charged:

> Mr. George William Curtis is himself the best illustration of the timidity, as of the patriotism and purity of this class, who need only bravery to give them the command they may have if they will. . . . Each year he has protested nobly;

8. Ernest Samuels, introduction to Henry Adams, *Democracy* and *Esther* (Garden City: Doubleday, 1961), xiv, and 42, 194, 201; Edward Chalfant perversely contends that Adams never intended Radcliffe to represent Blaine; see his *Better in Darkness: A Biography of Henry Adams, His Second Life, 1862–1891*, 410, 806–9; Chalfant also guesses the novel was completed in 1876; see p. 777.

9. In 1884, Henry was more engaged in building a new house in Washington than in organizing an independent campaign. He said, "we can afford to let our juniors try their hands at it"; Henry Adams to Gaskell, May 18, 1884, *Letters of Henry Adams*, 2:539. For a dismissal of Adams, see Ray Ginger, *Age of Excess* (New York: Macmillan, 1975), 134–36.

each year—until now—when the time came to act; he has 'knuckled down.' He didn't know he would; but the politicians did.

The specific election that created Bowker's outrage occurred in 1879 when New York Senator Conkling manipulated the Republican primary to gain absolute control of the state's party convention, naming his slate of candidates, including two whose graft seemed especially obnoxious. Bowker responded by calling for independents to "scratch" the two most offensive candidate names while voting for the other party nominees. Bowker created both publicity and organization, printing thousands of alternative Republican ballots with blank spaces for governor and state engineer. Bowker's campaign secured twenty thousand scratchers who proved themselves 5 percent of the Republican vote and numerous enough to cast the balance of power and, in this election, to defeat the state engineer.[10]

New York scratchers and Massachusetts reformers attended the 1880 Republican presidential convention to prevent either General Grant or James G. Blaine from gaining the nomination. The two spoilsmen blocked each other, permitting the selection of James Garfield. The election of an Ohio congressman with a Williams College moral education, long connections with independents, and membership in the Cobden Club persuaded reformers that they held the balance of power between the two parties. As Charles Francis Adams Jr. explained in the *Nation,* in a vote of nine million, General Garfield won by the narrow plurality of three thousand votes. A change of one vote in a hundred in New York or most any northeast state would have changed the outcome of the election. Independents claimed that their votes saved the election for Garfield, and they expected both parties to bid for their support in the future.[11]

Independents and their press were gaining strength. The *Nation* had long published on the edge of bankruptcy, but in 1881 it achieved financial health when the railroad capitalist and liberal Henry Villard bought the *Nation* for $40,000 and the *New York Evening Post* for $900,000, combining the weekly and the daily newspaper under the same reform editors. While Villard remained majority owner, large blocks of shares in the *Evening Post* were sold to the editors and their liberal friends, including David A. Wells and Henry Adams, who invested $20,000. Villard intended Carl Schurz

10. E. McClung Fleming, *R. R. Bowker: Militant Liberal,* 86, 90–91, 106, 115–17, 122.
11. Charles Francis Adams Jr., "The Opposition and the Unknown Quantity in Politics," *Nation* 32 (Feb. 14, 1881): 111; E. L. Godkin, "General Garfield and the Bosses," *Nation* 32 (Feb. 24, 1881): 124.

to be editor-in-chief with Horace White and E. L. Godkin as associate editors. But agreement on liberal principles did not restrain Godkin's ego from refusing to take second place. By the fall of 1883, he ousted the more kindly Schurz from the editorship. Godkin and Horace White remained to edit the leading paper of an increasingly confident community of liberal readers.[12]

Independents actually had spoilsmen on the run after the assassination of President Garfield in 1881, by a disappointed office seeker, gave reformers a winning issue. The message that spoils politics was murder turned voters against Republican spoilsmen in the elections of 1882, producing Democratic victories and conversions to civil service reform by surviving Republican politicians. Spoilsmen hated being forced to vote for the Pendleton Act, but believed they could no longer resist reform. And Henry Adams reported with glee, "the average congressman . . . is now chiefly occupied in swearing at professional reformers and voting for their bills."[13]

The Mugwump bolt occurred because Republican politicians stopped bidding for those independent votes in their national convention in 1884. Mugwumps were outraged and shocked by Republican disdain for independent voters; party leaders chose James G. Blaine, who had long been most obnoxious to the independents. The charismatic Republican from Maine had entered politics as an antislavery Republican and even misled independents into thinking he was one of them, but in 1872, he had refused to support the independent movement. Blaine possessed personality but no principle. He could not be counted on to stand firm for any of the reform principles. He was a spoilsman, as E. L. Godkin said, who "wallowed in spoils like a rhinoceros in an African pool." And as Speaker of the House he had taken the railroad bond bribe, which became widely publicized in the Mulligan letters. Blaine himself represented the corruption that independents opposed, and his nomination a triumph of the corrupt element in the Republican party. To support Blaine was unthinkable for an independent.[14]

---

12. Armstrong, *E. L. Godkin: A Biography*, 140–58.

13. Henry Adams to John Hay, Jan. 7, 1883, *Letters of Henry Adams*, 2:487–88.

14. Henry had written in 1882, "our pet enmity is Mr. Blaine. . . . His overthrow has been a matter of deep concern to us, both politically and personally, for we have always refused him even social recognition on account of his previous scandals . . ."; Adams to Gaskell, Jan. 29, 1882, *Letters of Henry Adams*, 2:448. E. L. Godkin, "The Republican Ticket and Platform," *Nation* 38 (June 12, 1884): 500; Logsdon, *Horace White*, 302–7.

Only an independent more concerned with building a career in politics than with reform could remain in the Republican party. Two such ambitious young independents were Henry Cabot Lodge of Massachusetts and Theodore Roosevelt of New York, who had been convention leaders against Blaine. When their bloc of ninety delegates failed to stop the nomination of the spoilsman, both were bitter and Roosevelt felt inclined to bolt, telling the *Nation* executive, Horace White, "any proper Democratic nominee will have our hearty support." But on sober reflection, the two independents decided their political future required party loyalty. Lodge sought a party nomination for Congress and discarded Henry Adams's old advice, choosing party and position over principle. Of course, the two deserting independents defended their honor, saying principle required them to support the nominee no matter how unwise. Their fellow independents had no tolerance for such opportunism. The Massachusetts Reform Club quickly assembled the day after the Blaine nomination, and repudiated Lodge for selling his soul and sacrificing principle for expediency. Lodge lost virtually all his independent friends. President Charles Eliot of Harvard College and respectable Boston reformers grimly condemned Lodge's failure to stand for principle and resolved to bolt his Republican party. New York independents followed the Boston initiative, meeting on June 18, with Carl Schurz and George William Curtis, to call for an independent Republican bolt.[15]

When Democrats selected Governor Grover Cleveland on July 11 for their presidential candidate, independents called a New York City convention of anti-Blaine reformers to organize and win Republican voters to the Democratic candidate. Cleveland lacked a college education or any observable political skills, and yet he won independent admiration for the enemies he had made, the machine politicians who hated him. As governor of New York he declared war on the Tammany Hall machine, which had endeared him to reformers who hated Democratic city machines as much as they detested the Republican patronage machine. Cleveland was a frugal administrator with an anticorruption record; and as a Democrat he could be expected to push tariff reform, which no Republican had ever done. A vote for Cleveland would be a vote to punish Republicans, a vote for tariff reform, and a vote against corruption.[16]

15. Elting E. Morison, John Blum, and John J. Buckley, eds., *The Letters of Theodore Roosevelt,* 1:70–72; Garraty, *Henry Cabot Lodge,* 78–86; Henry Cabot Lodge, *Selections from the Correspondence of Theodore Roosevelt and Henry Cabot Lodge, 1884–1918* (New York: Charles Scribner's, 1925), 11–12.

16. George Haven Putnam, *Memories of a Publisher, 1865–1915,* 95–98; Henry Adams to Gaskell, Sept. 21, 1884, *Letters of Henry Adams,* 2:551.

Unfortunately the campaign became diverted from independent issues when Republicans discovered that the unmarried Cleveland had once taken a mistress, a widow with two teenage children, and probably fathered an illegitimate child. Republicans had their moral issue of chastity and pushed it hard in small-town America. Evangelical Protestants in the North probably judged the sin of sexual promiscuity damaging enough to vote against Cleveland. However, the more secular independents judged private chastity a less important virtue in a politician than financial honesty; but although they would have preferred to avoid the personal issues and promote their old trilogy of issues, public character was determined to be the winning issue. Henry Adams laughed about the avoidance of real issues:

> We are here plunged in politics funnier than words can express. Very great issues are involved. Especially everyone knows that a step towards free trade is inevitable if the democrats come in. For the first time in twenty-eight years, a democratic administration is almost inevitable. The public is angry and abusive. Everyone takes part. We are all doing our best, and swearing at each other like demons. But the amusing thing is that no one talks about real interests. By common consent they agree to let these alone. We are afraid to discuss them. Instead of this, the press is engaged in a most amusing dispute whether Mr. Cleveland had an illegitimate child, and did or did not live with more than one mistress; whether Mr. Blaine got paid in railway bonds for services as Speaker; and whether Mrs. Blaine had a baby three months after her marriage. Nothing funnier than some of these subjects had been treated in my time. . . . Society is torn to pieces. Parties are wrecked from top to bottom. A great political revolution seems impending.[17]

The issues of importance to Henry Adams were those to which he and other independents had been committed for almost two decades. Yet stylish new interpretations of Mugwump motivation have been proposed by recent historians. For example, the Mugwumps were just young professionals, the product of modernization, we have been told. Gerald W. McFarland constructed a socioeconomic profile of 429 New York bolters. The quantified composite portrait of a college-educated professional and business Mugwump permitted the imaginative interpretation that these were modernizers, a new professional and bureaucratic generation that saw Blaine as a threat to professionalism. This creative

17. Adams to Gaskell, Sept. 21, 1884, *Letters of Henry Adams*, 2:551.

interpretation can quote no Mugwump who believed he was bolting for modernization. Bolters thought not in the language of law or bureaucracy, but in the language of moral philosophy. Mugwumpery grew not from new professionalization, but from old concerns of corrupt and abusive government.[18]

The difference between a bolter and a regular Republican might be illustrated by two New York City immigrants who bet a hat on the outcome of the election. One voted tradition and self-interest, and the other hope and moral principle. Andrew Carnegie, the steel capitalist who had come to America as a penniless Scot with a fourth-grade education, bet on Blaine and the Republicans whose protective tariff had provided generous price supports for Carnegie Steel. E. L. Godkin, the Scotch-Irish immigrant with the college education, had been taught that the spoils system and the protective tariff were damaging to the common good. Godkin, editor of the *Nation* and the *New York Post,* won the new hat by supporting Cleveland, whose victory promised to support free-market economics and strike a blow against Republican corruption.[19]

"Corruption," a key word in Mugwump vocabulary, expressed reformer repugnance with past Republican expediency on civil service, money, and tariff questions. Political concessions to special interests, at the expense of the general welfare, were considered corruption. Long before Blaine took railroad bonds, his accommodation of patronage spoils, protective tariffs, and silver coinage were regarded as evidence of corruption by Mugwumps. When the Republican national convention of 1884 rejected the moral ethics of Mugwumps by nominating Blaine, Democratic candidate Grover Cleveland became the hope of the New York Mugwumps, who signed an organizing manifesto declaring their belief in civil service reform, an end to silver coinage, and tariff reform.[20]

All the old independents were committed to liberal economics, and the new Mugwumps were, too. The memoirs of the Young Scratcher George H. Putnam tell a typical story of joining the Free Trade League in the 1870s to propagandize against Republican tariff protection. "It was our hope," Putnam said, "that as the youngsters came out of college from year to year, with the kind of knowledge of the history of economics that

18. The professional-impulse case is made by Gerald W. McFarland, *Mugwumps, Morals, and Politics, 1884–1920,* 38–50, who also retains the "public morality" explanation.
19. E. L. Godkin to Andrew Carnegie, Nov. 7, 1884, in Armstrong, *Gilded Age Letters of E. L. Godkin,* 316.
20. Fleming, *R. R. Bowker,* 204.

would be given to them by professors like W. G. Sumner of Yale, we should gradually secure a larger hold on public opinion. . . ."[21]

Mugwump professor William Graham Sumner taught that Republican protectionism existed as a "shameful," "ignorant" remnant of despotic exploitation from the past. Restrictions on trade were a little like human slavery—both deprived individuals of part of the fruits of their labor. Not only did consumers pay more because of tariffs, but the practice corrupted the political system. The protection policy originated in graft; capitalists solicited special protection from Congress to enlarge their profits. Only with the abolition of corrupt protection would Congress become friendly to reform.[22]

The young Mugwumps Sumner, Bowker, and Putnam shared the Adam Smith liberalism of the older Mugwumps David A. Wells, Edward L. Godkin, and Edward Atkinson. Bowker organized Mugwumps into his Society for Political Education in 1880, publishing free-market books such as Arthur L. Perry, *Introduction to Political Economy* (1880) and using these cheap books and pamphlets to promote reading circles, lecture series, and forums for discussion. Bowker wrote his own regular column, "Plain Talks on Economics," for a weekly free-trade paper, *The Million,* published in Iowa. He and his Mugwump associates, such as David A. Wells, Horace White, Charles Francis Adams Jr., and William Graham Sumner, were all part of a popular-education campaign that lasted more than a decade.[23]

Mugwumps hoped for much more than the negative goal of defeating Blaine because he lacked public virtue. They wanted to make the two-party system work again by forcing politicians to pay attention to the issues— tariff, civil service, and currency reform. The connection between the Cleveland campaign and liberal economics is illustrated by the Harvard professor of political economy who took a leave of absence to direct the *Boston Daily Advertiser* editorial campaign for Grover Cleveland. Professor Charles F. Dunbar had edited the paper in the 1860s, before President Charles W. Eliot of Harvard recruited him to fill the college's first chair of political economy. Dunbar used Adam Smith's *Wealth of Nations* and John Stuart Mill's *Political Economy* to teach the classical theory that legislatures were unfit to regulate the money system or the trade of a nation. Certainly he admitted, as did all Mugwumps, that laissez-faire was not a

---

21. Putnam, *Memories of a Publisher,* 42–43.
22. William Graham Sumner, *Lectures on the History of Protection* (New York: Putnam's, 1877).
23. Fleming, *R. R. Bowker,* 101–3, 213, 221.

scientific law, but it was "a handy rule of practice." In the election of 1884, Professor Dunbar thought Cleveland stood closer to liberal economic wisdom than Blaine.[24]

The wisdom of deserting the Republican party in hopes of achieving reform had always been questioned by practical politicians who insisted that nothing could be achieved outside a party. Those professionals had been right in 1872; the Liberal Republican campaign accomplished nothing that year. But reformer efforts inside the Republican party had also achieved nothing in the twenty years since the Civil War. Reformers reasonably concluded that nothing could be accomplished by continuing to work within a party dominated by patronage and corruption. Party independence offered the only realistic hope of changing politics. With the two parties so evenly matched in votes, reformers believed they could gain recognition for their issues if they proved numerous enough to elect Cleveland to the presidency.

New York Mugwumps offered Theodore Roosevelt a chance to reconsider and join them in reform, insisting:

> You are separating yourself now from great possibilities of good work. The regular Republicans do not want you any more than the regular Democrats want us Independent Republicans. Your power is gone when you forego principle for party, and those who have been associated with you have had in this campaign no more sincere sorrow than the feeling that in the hope of success 'within the party' you have surrendered the one possibility of continuing the work for which your name has been respected throughout the country.[25]

Roosevelt defended his and Henry Cabot Lodge's party loyalty by a vigorous attack on the shameful Civil War record of the Democratic party.[26] But "waving the bloody shirt" from the Civil War failed Roosevelt and the Republican party in 1884.

---

24. J. Laurence Laughlin, "Charles Franklin Dunbar," *Journal of Political Economy* 8 (Mar. 1900): 237–38; Charles Eliot, "Charles Franklin Dunbar," *Massachusetts Historical Society Proceedings* 13 (Feb. 1900): 429–37; Edward H. Hall, "Memoir," *Massachusetts Historical Society Proceedings* 14 (June 1900): 218–24; F. W. Taussig, introduction to *Economic Essays of Charles Franklin Dunbar,* ed. O. M. W. Sprague (New York: Macmillan, 1904).

25. Fleming, *R. R. Bowker,* 209.

26. Lodge, *Selections from the Correspondence of Theodore Roosevelt and Henry Cabot Lodge,* 1:24–25.

Delighted Mugwumps were certain that the Civil War period in American politics had finally ended. And the election turned on such a small margin that Mugwumps could claim their votes determined the election. Cleveland had won the state of New York by a mere 1,149 votes. So the *Nation* declared: "The Independent Republicans of the country have elected Grover Cleveland President. That point is so clear in the results that nobody questions it."[27] Mugwumps rejoiced that they had decided a presidential election, and the political parties would finally be forced to take their economic liberalism seriously.

27. "The Week," *Nation* 39 (Nov. 13, 1884): 407; Godkin to James Bryce, Nov. 23, 1884, in Armstrong, *Gilded Age Letters of E. L. Godkin;* twentieth-century scholars have disparaged the role of independent voting; see Geoffrey Blodgett, "The Mugwump Reputation, 1870 to the Present," 873–75; for the political science realism of Angus Campbell et al., see their work *The American Voter* (New York: Wiley 1960), 143–45; this view was also adopted by the historians Sproat, *The "Best" Men,* and John M. Dobson, *Politics in the Gilded Age* (New York: Praeger, 1972), 165. An opposite thesis—Mugwump success with educational politics ruined the great partisan party system—is developed by Michael E. McGerr, *The Decline of Popular Politics: The American North, 1865–1928.*

8

Reforming the Democratic Party

For two decades Mugwumps censured Republicans and Democrats as cultural, tribal factions rather than parties of principle. Scholarly laments of Woodrow Wilson and James Bryce were representative indictments. Both parties lacked moral principle, Wilson declared in *Congressional Government* (1885): "Each tolerates all sorts of difference of creed and variety of aim within its own ranks. . . . They are like armies without officers, engaged upon a campaign which has no great cause." James Bryce agreed, in *American Commonwealth* (1888), concluding, "neither party has any principles, any distinctive tenets." Parties campaigned for office by appealing to traditions, interests, and organization, not by commitment to great principles.[1] The Mugwump hope for a party of principle remained unfulfilled until the election of 1888.

For liberals who had come of age in the abolitionist struggle and achieved freedom through Lincoln Republicans, the capture of their party by political professionals was one of the most outrageous crimes of the age. To recover the party from professionals and their spoils system of assessing government employees, reformers designed civil service reform. After their disappointment with Grant, reformers returned to the issue, organizing local and national civil service reform leagues. President Garfield's assassination by a disappointed office seeker in 1881 gave reform a simple illustration that the spoils system equaled murder.[2] Congress

---

1. Woodrow Wilson, *Congressional Government,* reprinted in Arthur S. Link, ed., *The Papers of Woodrow Wilson* (Princeton: Princeton University Press, 1968), 4:13–179; James Bryce, *The American Commonwealth,* ed. Louis M. Hacker, vol. 1 (New York: G. P. Putnam, 1959), 151; neither scholar was a Mugwump, but their sources were.
2. Hoogenboom, *Outlawing the Spoils,* 179–97, 212–15, 253.

finally capitulated to popular opinion in 1883, passing the Pendleton Act. Reformers had hoped to liberate the political organization and return it to its tradition as the party of principle. But legislating civil service reform in 1883 simply hastened the shift of financing for Republican professionals from office holders to protected manufacturers, pushing any possibility of tariff reform entirely out of the party.[3]

Before the 1880s, all Republican presidents spoke of the need for tariff reform. In 1868, a Republican congressman, James A. Garfield, had even proudly accepted membership in the free-trade British Cobden Club. But such liberal opinion ceased to be tolerated as protected manufacturers became the financial supporters of the party. The tariff became sacred and the Cobden Club demonic. Protective duties grew to be the core Republican belief, the major policy creed of the party, the key test of whether a person was a Republican.[4]

The Republican transformation distressed liberals, who had been tariff reformers ever since reading the inspiring story of Richard Cobden's twenty-year campaign to convert the British Whig party to tariff reform against the entrenched Tory interests. The victory of British tariff reform in 1846 and the British shift to free trade had been one of the great victories of western liberalism. Correspondence among Mugwumps in the 1870s and 1880s was peppered with references to Cobden and his friend Bright. Who would become the American Cobden to educate a political party against government interference in the marketplace? The most frequently mentioned candidate was David A. Wells, who turned to the Democratic party in the 1870s not for what it was, but for what it might become. But Wells never won the Democratic nomination for Congress in his state of Connecticut. His district unfortunately included manufacturers willing to mortgage their industrial plant to keep Wells out of Congress. So in the 1870s, Wells could only draft reform tariffs for House Speaker M. C. Kerr, pen reform speeches for Democratic congressmen, pass out honorary memberships in the Cobden Club, and participate in programs for public education, which he hoped would move Democrats to liberate markets from government control.[5]

3. See my chapter 4, and Matthew Josephson, *The Politicos* (New York: Harcourt, Brace, 1938), 322–23; George H. Mayer, *The Republican Party* (New York: Oxford University Press, 1967), 215.
4. E. L. Godkin, "How Common Things Became Sacred," *Nation* 47 (Oct. 4, 1888): 262.
5. Watson Sperry to Wells, Sept. 20, 1876, reel 4, 2517–18; M. C. Kerr to Wells, Jan. 17, 1876, reel 4, 2058; W. M. Morrison to Wells, Apr. 5, 1877, reel 5, 2693–94, reel 5; Thomas

Wells worked with the New York City Free Trade Club to spread demands for tax and price reductions across the Midwest. Paid organizers built free-trade clubs across Ohio, Illinois, Michigan, and Iowa, supplying lecturers such as Wells and William Graham Sumner, and sending tons of free-trade propaganda. The financing came from contributors such as corporate attorney Thomas G. Shearman, a true believer who wanted an organization "such as Cobden and Bright carried on in England. . . ." Shearman shared the liberal independent vision. "I would rather belong to a little energetic, unselfish party, that did not expect to elect any of its own members to office, than to one of the great successful parties. I don't want office. . . . But I should immensely enjoy work with a compact, unpurchasable little party, that should force each of the big parties to shape action with reference to our demands."[6]

A second New York free trader, R. R. Bowker, worked with Wells to organize the Society for Political Education. Bowker, the publisher and liberal who had organized Adam Smith's centennial dinner in New York, used his new organization for nonprofit publishing of economic tracts by Edward Atkinson and Horace White and for a library of political economy by John Stuart Mill and David A. Wells. Bowker devoted half his time to unfunded reform work, publishing, speaking, and writing on economic liberalism. By 1884 his society funded a weekly free-trade paper, *The Million,* published in Des Moines, Iowa.[7]

Wells published his best work in serious journals and in *Recent Economic Changes* (1889), developing a sophisticated argument for reducing tariff walls as a means of avoiding American troubles of overproduction and economic depression. Dramatic world economic growth, resulting largely from new machinery, created rapidly falling prices and the promise of ending poverty. But American tariff walls, especially on raw materials, drove up manufacturing costs while pricing foreign-manufactured products out of the American market and denying the mutually advantageous exchange of goods. Tariff walls shrank the world market because nations retaliated with prohibitive restrictions against the goods of high-tariff

G. Shearman to Wells, Nov. 23, 1880, reel 6, 3465; Morrison to Wells, Jan. 14, 1882, reel 6, 3677; Edward Atkinson to Wells, Nov. 8, 1884, reel 7, 4072, Wells Papers; Tom Terrill, "David A. Wells, the Democracy, and Tariff Reduction, 1877–1894," 540–55.

6. Alfred B. Mason to Wells, July 29, 1876, reel 4, 2432; J. P. Townsend to Wells, Apr. 21, 1877, reel 5, 2714; Shearman to Wells, July 8, 1882, reel 6, 3730–32, Wells Papers.

7. R. R. Bowker to Wells, June 12, 1880, reel 6, 3387–88, Wells Papers; Fleming, *R. R. Bowker,* 211–21.

nations. American manufacturers were certainly able to compete without any special protection, Wells said, arguing that freer trade would enlarge the size of the market for American goods. Lower tariff duties on foreign raw materials would make U.S. industries more competitive by lowering costs for products manufactured from foreign parts. If foreigners were permitted to sell in the American market, Wells said, they would have money to purchase more American manufactured products. All could gain from freer trade.[8]

The Wells economic argument enjoyed overwhelming support among college political economists as well as the most popular economic writer, Henry George, whose *Progress and Poverty* (1879) had become the best-selling economic book. While Wells objected to George's special idea of the single tax on land, George was an enthusiastic free trader who applauded the work of Wells and the Society for Political Education. "I want all you want and more," George wrote, "and it will be a long time before we get where you want to stop." "I am a free trader pure and absolute, and regard protection as a fraud on workingmen."[9]

In the colleges, even "new" economists agreed with the liberal de-nunciation of protection. German-educated Richard T. Ely and Henry Carter Adams had no desire to enrich manufacturers; they agreed with classical political economy on the error of protection. But free trade was not a pressing issue for the new economists; their passion was for the distribution of wealth to workers, and they left the tariff debate to the liberals. The only protectionist center of thought seemed to be in Pennsylvania, where the protected metal manufacturer Joseph Wharton had donated $100,000 to establish the first business school to counter the teachings of classical political economy. Professor Simon N. Patten taught the protection doctrine at Pennsylvania University's Wharton School.[10]

The Pennsylvania protectionists also held controlling influence in both political parties. The Republican party had endorsed a higher tariff in the 1850s to win Pennsylvania votes. And Pennsylvanians prevented the Democratic party from legislating tariff reform through their Philadelphia congressman, Samuel J. Randall. Randall entered Congress in 1862 from a commercial, manufacturing district and for thirty years he headed a bloc of Democrats from northern industrial districts who supported tariff

8. Tom E. Terrill, *The Tariff, Politics, and American Foreign Policy, 1874–1901*, 58–60.
9. Henry George to Wells, Dec. 9, 1880, reel 6, 3491; Dec. 12, 1883, reel 7, 3861–62; Oct. 12, 1886, reel 7, 4224, Wells Papers.
10. Joanne Reitano, *The Tariff Question in the Gilded Age*, 34–35, 52.

protection, killing virtually every reform effort. As a three-time Speaker of the House in the 1870s, he retained the clout to kill the Morrison 20 percent reduction bill in 1884 by leading 41 Democrats to vote with Republicans against tariff reduction.[11]

Political corruption by manufacturing interests came to be regarded by Mugwumps as even more dangerous to America than the economic damage of higher prices. Mugwumps began to compare protection with the old evil of slavery as a corrupter of political institutions. Just as the Democratic party had been taken over by slave interests before the war, so did the new manufacturers seem to have captured the Republican party. The most distinctive change in American life had been the rise to dominance of the manufacturing capitalists, whose fortunes had been guaranteed by tariff legislation. And the new millionaires made the Senate a capitalists' club, where the manufacturers protected their property with every legislative weapon within their reach.[12]

In the 1880s, protection created monopoly combinations that ruthlessly used their enormous wealth to control the political system. Of the more than forty trusts that the Mugwump Horace White counted in 1888, virtually all, he said, resulted from tariff protection. Only three exceptions—Standard Oil, Cotton Seed Oil, and the Whiskey Trust—were identified by White as having no special government assistance; those three developed from a natural American monopoly of a raw material that did not exist abroad. All other trusts, White said, could be broken by reduced tariffs to permit foreign competition. The typical trust—the American Sugar Refining Company—could not exist if American politicians did not legislate it a monopoly of the American market. Mugwumps clearly embraced the popular slogan that "the tariff is the mother of trusts."[13]

For three years Mugwumps advised President Grover Cleveland to take on protection. For three years he hesitated. Then on December 6, 1887, Cleveland devoted his entire Annual Message to an attack on the "vicious, inequitable, and illogical" tariff. Government revenues exceeded expenses by $55 million, Cleveland told Congress, and might double the following

11. H. Wayne Morgan, *From Hayes to McKinley: National Party Politics*, 81–82, 169, 271; Terrill, *Tariff, Politics, and American Foreign Policy*, 100.

12. William Graham Sumner, *Protectionism* (New York: Henry Holt, 1885), 165; E. L. Godkin, "A Retrospect," *Nation* 51 (July 3, 1890): 4–5.

13. Horace White, "Trusts," *Nation* 47 (Aug. 16, 1888): 125; for a survey of the rise of trusts, see Hans B. Thorelli, *The Federal Antitrust Policy* (Baltimore: Johns Hopkins Press, 1955), 72–85.

year to $110 million, creating an enormous surplus of cash in the treasury possibly damaging both to the economy and to the morality of Congress. A tariff that raised unnecessary funds for the benefit of manufacturers, creating trusts at the expense of consumers, could no longer be defended. Congress must reduce duties on the necessities of life and on raw materials used in manufacturing, Cleveland said. Tariff reform would give the nation cheaper manufacturing costs, lower consumer prices, and greater foreign exports.[14]

Cleveland never played clever politics with the tariff; he was too slow of mind and speech for manipulating voters. His "rapid and freakish" rise to power had come from direct and straightforward vetoes of graft, not through political maneuvers. The support of Mugwumps had been essential to his election in 1884, and he needed their political support again. Relations with Mugwumps had deteriorated seriously when he handed out Democratic patronage appointments. Cleveland would never be able to please reformers on civil service, but he could give them the campaign for tariff reform they wanted. Besides, his favorite cabinet officer, William F. Vilas, as well as secretaries Thomas F. Bayard and Daniel Manning, were tariff reformers in good standing with David A. Wells.[15]

The 1887 tariff message restored President Cleveland's character with Mugwumps. E. L. Godkin could forget Cleveland's past "lapses from virtue" and praise his new tariff message as the "first real state paper" since the presidency of Abraham Lincoln.[16] The fabled Mugwump admiration of Cleveland really began with this bold message, which turned protection into the central political issue for the next five years. Cleveland became the Mugwump hero when he gave them a real debate on the tariff by committing his party to reform.

The great debate began April 17, 1888, with Texas Democrat and Chairman of the House Ways and Means Committee, Roger Q. Mills, charging that special privilege divided America into two classes, the rich and the poor. The Mills critique of manufacturing wealth sounded much

14. Reitano, *Tariff Question*, 6–11; George F. Parker, ed., *The Writings and Speeches of Grover Cleveland* (New York: Cassell, 1892), 72–87.

15. A cynical revisionist "explained" Cleveland's tariff turn as a diversion to turn voters against trade unionism; see Geoffrey Blodgett, *The Gentle Reformers: Massachusetts Democrats in the Cleveland Era*, 79–80. Horace White to Wells, Jan. 1887, reel 7, 4246, Wells Papers; Joyner, *David Ames Wells*, 167–68; Terrill, "David A. Wells," 553; Horace S. Merrill, *William Freeman Vilas: Doctrinaire Democrat* (Madison: State Historical Society of Wisconsin, 1954), 78, 131–32.

16. E. L. Godkin, "The Effect of the Message," *Nation* 46 (Jan. 19, 1888): 44.

like the rhetoric of Texas Alliance populists, even though the Mills reform would lower tariff rates only a modest 7 percent. The strong leadership of Mills and President Cleveland reduced Representative Randall's forty protection votes to only four. Democrats no longer dared to break with their party and vote against reform. The Mills bill passed the House only to be blocked by the Republican Senate and debated in the elections of 1888.[17]

Grover Cleveland staked his Democratic future on reform in 1888, while alarmed manufacturers donated an unprecedented $3 million for the Republican Benjamin Harrison's campaign fund to block any roll back of protection. Voters shifted to Grover Cleveland, increasing his vote and giving him eighty thousand more popular votes than the Republican candidate, but still failing to secure the important electoral vote. It was in this election that Republican fund-raiser Senator Matthew Quay was reported to have confessed to buying votes and the election, saying that Harrison "would never know how close a number of men were compelled to approach the gates of the penitentiary to make him President."[18]

Cleveland lost the election of 1888, but Mugwumps were certain moral virtue had returned to politics. The tariff had become a live issue engaging public attention. Just as in the days of the old slavery debates, reformers believed they were riding the crest of inevitable reform. They were destined to win. The fight against the "wicked system" had finally begun and could only expand until tariff robbery and plunder were defeated. The financial editor of the *Nation,* Horace White, even suggested that congressional Democrats stand back and let the new Republican Congress enact a new and even more protective tariff to reveal the true corruption of Republicans. Now that Republicans were governed by trusts and combinations, the party should be permitted to show its real character to the public. So Mugwumps took a perverse delight in watching Republicans legislate the new McKinley tariff of 1890, a bonanza for manufacturers, which raised the average level to 50 percent.[19]

The following election promised to be all that the Mugwumps had hoped. President Harrison and his Republican party were forced to defend the highest tariff in American history and they rashly defended higher consumer prices. "I cannot find myself in sympathy with this demand for cheaper coats," President Harrison said, "which seems to me necessarily

17. Reitano, *Tariff Question,* 19–22.
18. Josephson, *Politicos,* 433; Morgan, *From Hayes to McKinley,* 319.
19. Horace White, "Retrospect and Prospect," *Nation* 47 (Nov. 8, 1888): 368; Horace White, "An Extra Session," *Nation* 47 (Dec. 20, 1888): 490.

to involve a cheaper man and woman under the coat." Republicans should have known politicians never win by advocating extravagance rather than frugality and thrift. Voters certainly did not want to hear that America was "not a cheap country" and that the more they paid for necessities the happier they would be.[20]

The *Nation* took a perverse delight in catching Massachusetts Republican Henry Cabot Lodge in the act of defending his party's "anti-cheap coat" tariff argument. Lodge had been despised by Mugwumps ever since he sold his soul for party politics and supported Blaine in 1884. The young reformer had been one of Henry Adams's free trade independents until he entered politics. Now he offered the best example of why independent young men should not enter politics. The former free trader now supported protection with arguments that a Harvard-trained Ph.D. in history could never have believed. "The cry for cheapness is unamerican," Lodge said, "and there is such a thing as too much cheapness." Lodge was the perfect example of Moorfield Storey's message to Harvard men that in nine out of ten cases, the young office seeker sacrificed character just to get into office, and once elected to Congress, the percentage of corruption rose higher.[21]

The old tariff defense of claiming that protection assisted employees as well as manufacturers would not work in the election of 1892. Only a seventh of workers were in protected industries. And workers in those industries now knew that while prices had gone up under the McKinley tariff, wages had not. McKinley gave the iron and steel industry all the protection requested, but multiple wage reductions and strikes, including Andrew Carnegie's union-busting Homestead disaster, had followed.[22]

The elections of 1892 proved a triumph for Grover Cleveland, Democrats, and tariff reform. The Cleveland antitariff message, which looked like a Mugwump failure in 1888, now turned into a stroke of genius for 1892. Freedom from oppression by the trusts had become a winning issue. And the president who had led this emancipation from trusts and combinations was now ranked with George Washington and Abraham Lincoln by the Mugwumps. In fact, they went further and placed Cleveland beside Martin Luther, a simple man of truth who had begun the Protestant

20. E. L. Godkin, "Cheapness," *Nation* 51 (Oct. 23, 1890): 316.

21. Ibid.; E. L. Godkin, "Saving Truths for Young Politicians," *Nation* 47 (Oct. 25, 1888): 326–27.

22. Horace White, "Mutatis Mutandis," *Nation* 51 (Oct. 30, 1890): 337–38; Rollo Ogden, "Forcing the Fighting in the Senate," *Nation* 55 (July 7, 1892): 4.

Reformation, declaring: "Here I stand. I can do no otherwise. God help me."[23] Cleveland seemed a noble reformer of simple courage and sound doctrine, and his tariff struggle made him the heroic Mugwump politician.

For a brief moment after the 1892 elections, Cleveland Democrats promised to be a free-trade party. But the financial panic of 1893 diverted Cleveland from tariff to currency reform, repealing the Sherman Silver Purchase Act. Cleveland's silver repeal drove Democrats of the West and South into rebellion against Eastern leadership and into an alliance with populist inflation remedies for relieving agricultural distress. When Cleveland turned to eliminating protection in 1894 with the Wilson-Gorman tariff, he had lost the clout to strip the trusts of their protection or to eliminate duties from raw materials.[24] Democrats disappointed the Mugwumps, failing to become the party of liberal principle and failing to remain in power. In fact, it would be twenty more years, in the Woodrow Wilson administration, before Democrats finally returned to power and stripped tariff protection from American trusts.

23. E. L. Godkin, "A Great Example," *Nation* 55 (Nov. 10, 1892): 346; W. P. Garrison, "The Third Stage of Our Industrial Enfranchisement," *Nation* 55 (Nov. 17, 1892): 366.
24. Richard E. Welch Jr., *The Presidencies of Grover Cleveland*, 129–37.

9

Defeating Silver

The epic Mugwump struggle to preserve public virtue was the battle against silver dollars. The 1890s currency debates culminated a generation of opposition to a politically controlled money supply. While other groups, political parties, manufacturers, and farmers shifted positions on greenbacks and silver, Mugwumps consistently taught the classic wisdom from political economy that congressmen should never be trusted to change prices and values. Corruption, they insisted, naturally resulted when politicians legislated money for dominant interests. The public good could best be protected by a neutral government that permitted world markets to select the money and delegated management of paper currency and credit to the bankers. Mugwumps wanted to take money away from Congress and give it to bankers, which eventually happened with the Federal Reserve System of 1913, but not until the Mugwumps had helped defeat congressional efforts to inflate the money supply.[1]

The currency wars of the 1890s were much like those of the 1860s, except that political economy professors no longer unanimously sided with Mugwumps. A younger school of economists now criticized assumptions of the classical economists, and even a couple of Mugwumps went over to the new thought. Young German-educated professors broke with traditional liberal political economy in 1885 and established the American Economics Association, which proclaimed the old doctrines of laissez-faire "unsafe in politics and unsound in morals." These new scholars—Richard T. Ely, Edmund J. James, and Simon N. Patten—subscribed to

---

1. Mugwump support for "modern" bank paper began with Harvard professor Charles F. Dunbar's *Chapters on Banking* (1885), which argued national banknotes should be based on bank assets, which would permit an elastic currency capable of expanding with the requirements of business; see Dorfman, *Economic Mind in American Civilization*, 3:65–66.

the German historical school of economy. They believed that the world had known many stages of economic development, and the existing competitive system was just another temporary stage. In fact, they said, a new economic era already approached as advanced peoples transferred a great variety of businesses—from the printing of money to the operation of railways—to government management.[2]

The new school taught that social evolution required perpetual discovery of new economic truths; no economic laws were permanent, and each was applicable only to a particular stage of development. Laissez-faire had represented Adam Smith's rejection of excessive restrictions in a mercantilist state, but with the maturation of industrial civilization, the complexity of society made laissez-faire impracticable. The let-alone principle had created excessive inequalities in the distribution of wealth; it had allowed the strong to abuse the weak, and so, the new school critics said, the old principles of classical economics must be discarded and new laws discovered, laws that would effectively promote the general welfare.

The new school criticism, and the young professors, were dismissed by Mugwumps as soft-headed, tender-minded humanitarians who disliked the suffering that existed in a free economy. They were more social gospel theologians than scientists, E. L. Godkin said. And it was true that Reverend Washington Gladden and twenty-two other social gospel ministers were among the charter members of the new American Economics Association. To believe that the right amount of state interference could ever abolish poverty was pure utopianism to a tough-minded Mugwump such as Godkin, who pointed to the Tammany Hall political machine in New York politics and to the millionaires in the U.S. Senate as evidence that local and national governments had proven themselves untrustworthy to manage money. The test of a science, Godkin insisted, was its ability to predict with accuracy; any system of economics that disregarded the facts of political corruption and the base desire of most individuals to get as much as possible with a minimum of effort was no science.[3]

2. For the new school, see Fine, *Laissez Faire and the General Welfare State*, 198–251; Daniel M. Fox, *The Discovery of Abundance: Simon N. Patten and the Transformation of Social Theory* (Ithaca: Cornell University Press, 1967), 32–43; and Benjamin G. Rader, *The Academic Mind and Reform: The Influence of Richard T. Ely in American Life* (Lexington: University Press of Kentucky, 1966), 28–53.
3. Charles F. Dunbar, "The Reaction in Political Economy," *Quarterly Journal of Political Economy* 1 (Oct. 1886): 1–26; E. L. Godkin, "The New German Political Economy," *Nation* 21 (Sept. 9, 1875): 161–62; Godkin, "The Economic Man," *North American Review* 153 (Oct. 1891): 490–503.

The U.S. Senate of Daniel Webster and Charles Sumner had been replaced by a rich man's club filled with silver-mine owners and manufacturing capitalists. Republicans were said to have created five new western states in 1889–1890 out of little more than silver mines and cattle ranches just to create ten rotten borough Republican seats. The Senate decline, Mugwumps charged, had been as severe as that of the British House of Lords. Both had ceased to serve any useful purpose. Rather than continuing to be a deliberating body of statesmen, the Senate had become a deal-making chamber of commerce, protecting the manufacturing and mining enterprises that had bought the senators their seats. Respect for the upper house of government had disappeared among the Mugwumps.[4]

One former independent claimed the problem was not just the politicians but also the Mugwumps. Francis A. Walker, a second-generation political economist who had worked with David A. Wells in the Treasury Department and written an article with Henry Adams, now complimented the German historical school. Walker was a sort of academic politician, becoming president of M.I.T., and said that he found good in both economic schools. President Walker, who also presided over Ely's American Economic Association, used his presidential forum in 1890 to denounce the monetary views of orthodox economists for discrediting all economists with the public. The public no longer listened to Mugwumps because they had foolishly denied greenbacks the status of money, and every worker knew that a greenback could be spent in any store. Mugwump economists had also offended the public sense by refusing to admit that the existence of an inadequate supply of money had contributed to the evil of falling prices. In going against the common sense of the people, Walker said, the old economists had impaired their influence, and one immediate result would be congressional legislation of more silver coinage.[5]

And Walker was certainly right about the "Billion Dollar Congress" of 1890. The newly elected Republican majority descended on Washington intent on more government intervention in the economy—a new and higher McKinley Tariff and a Sherman Silver Act. The silver legislation was a straight political deal. Eastern manufacturing protectionists, who

4. "The Object of Stealing Senators," *New York Times*, Apr. 18, 1890, 4; "The Senate Now and Then," *Springfield Republican*, Apr. 11, 1891, 4; "The Decline of the Senate," *New York Evening Post*, Aug. 4, 1893, 4.

5. Francis A. Walker, "The Tide of Economic Thought," *Proceedings of the American Economic Association* 6 (1891): 15–38.

lacked the votes to win their new tariff, bought the votes of Western silver-mining interests, whose product prices had slumped badly as the world deserted silver currency. The silver Republicans made protectionists the gift of a scandalously high McKinley Tariff, and protectionists returned the favor by doubling government silver purchases to 4.5 million ounces a month, virtually the entire silver production of American mines.[6]

While Mugwump journals and economists screamed about the Republican Congress "prostituting the legislative power to satisfy the appetites of silver mine owners," commercial and financial circles were silent and resigned to more silver. Wall Street even expressed enthusiasm that congressional doctoring of the currency would bring on a bull market. More cautious bankers might have questioned the wisdom of a new silver act but did not view silver legislation with alarm. Most agreed with the spokesman for Chase National Bank that "no harm would come of it."[7]

The Sherman silver purchase could be explained as a political compromise to avoid free coinage, the unlimited government buying of silver, that had passed in the Senate. The compromise, which avoided the extreme of free silver, gained applause from the majority and troubled only pessimistic Mugwumps, who worried over future currency troubles should government fill the treasury with silver and let gold reserves decline. The value of the government paper money—greenbacks and Treasury notes—had been maintained by a large gold reserve, which guaranteed that paper dollars could be exchanged for gold dollars. Any loss of confidence in the Treasury's ability to maintain the gold standard could lead to a run on the gold reserve and a severe currency crisis, with greenbacks falling to their silver bullion value.[8]

The predicted drain on the gold reserve began within a year, as the comfortable gold balance of almost $200 million declined to $118 million by the summer of 1891. To move for repeal of the Sherman Silver Act, the Mugwump Horace White and his financier Henry Villard rallied eastern bankers behind a third nomination of Grover Cleveland for the presidency.

---

6. Homer S. Socolofsky and Allan B. Spetter, *The Presidency of Benjamin Harrison*, 58–59.

7. "Expert Opinions on Proposed Silver Legislation," *Bradstreet's* 18 (May 24, 1890): 326; "A Threatened Outrage," *New York Times*, June 2, 1890, 4.

8. "The New Silver Bill," *New York Times*, July 9, 1890, 4; Horace White, "The Silver Compromise," *Nation* 51 (July 10, 1890): 24; "The New Silver Bill," *Springfield Republican*, July 10, 1890, 4; F. W. Taussig, "The Working of the New Silver Act," *Forum* 10 (Oct. 1890): 165–72.

Cleveland had publicly denounced free-silver sentiment in the Democratic party, making himself the hope of Mugwumps and the foe of western and southern silverites. With the support of the Mugwump press, bankers, and financiers, Cleveland won the nomination and the presidency. When the panic and run on specie brought the gold reserve below a safety level of $100 million, Cleveland called a special session of Congress to repeal the Sherman Act.[9]

Congress assembled in the August heat of 1893 to consider Cleveland's charge that repeal of the Sherman Silver Act would protect the gold standard, save American credit, and ease financial distress. The House of Representatives voted repeal within twenty days against noisy silver crusaders such as William Jennings Bryan and Richard Bland, but in the Senate, a two-month filibuster by western and southern silverites delayed repeal while Mugwumps fretted about the decline of the Senate. They felt energized by the crisis, however, for it had restored majority respect for their traditional monetary theory. In this battle, the business community sided mostly with the Mugwumps, joining them in ridiculing those Pennsylvania protection manufacturers who still believed a government expansion of the money supply to be the way to get the economy rolling again. As Horace White pointed out to the inflationists, silver had actually contracted the money supply; fear of the American dollar falling to the silver standard frightened foreign investors into taking their gold back to Europe and caused American depositors to withdraw their gold from banks, collapsing many banks and speculators in the following monetary contraction. Mugwumps rejected all silver arguments that currency expansion could help farmers and debtors; government efforts to manage the money supply only created suffering, Mugwumps insisted. And finally, in late October, the Senate passed the repeal bill forty-three to thirty-two.[10]

Mugwumps hoped to follow repeal with currency reform—eliminating government paper and delegating currency to the national banks. But Washington politicians were unwilling or unable to take up currency

9. Paul Studenski and Herman E. Krooss, *Financial History of the United States* (New York: McGraw-Hill, 1963), 217; Logsdon, *Horace White*, 334–36; Henry Villard, *Memoirs of Henry Villard* (Boston: Houghton Mifflin, 1904), 2:357–62.

10. Welch, *Presidencies of Grover Cleveland*, 118–19, 122–23; "The Decline of the Senate," *New York Evening Post*, Aug. 4, 1893, 4; "Contraction through Silver Coinage," *New York Times*, Aug. 21, 1893, 4; "Mr. Dolan's Club," *New York Times*, Aug. 26, 1893, 4; Horace White, "Exit Silver," *Nation* 57 (Nov. 2, 1893): 322.

reform because silver repeal in 1893 failed to finish the old inflation debate. As business confidence and the gold reserve failed to recover in the deepest depression of the whole nineteenth century, silver forces remained very much alive with support in all sections and parties. The silver-manufacturing alliance revived as Democratic tariff reform threatened industrial interests and Republican Henry Cabot Lodge proposed making a tariff war on the British to force them to endorse bimetallism in cooperation with the United States. Mugwumps were outraged by continued eastern support for silver and especially by those few professors and former Mugwumps who gave support to silver.[11]

The panic of 1893 had overwhelmed the speculating Adams brothers. Charles Francis Jr. had carried his brothers John and Brooks into the great western real estate boom, pursuing a bold borrow-and-buy in Kansas City and Spokane that suddenly turned disastrous in the financial contraction of 1893. The Adams brothers were suspended over the edge of bankruptcy; banks were calling in loans, and "men died like flies under the strain. . . ." In the financial crisis, Henry and Brooks turned against the gold standard, developing a wild theory that mixed the populist creditor conspiracy notion with Darwinian-based ideas, declaring that Jews and bankers had captured control of the western world and abolished one-half of the currency—silver—to double the value of their gold at the expense of producers. This grim, dark theory would be spelled out in Brooks's *The Law of Civilization and Decay* (1895). The crisis-minded Adams brothers predicted a revolution against the contracting capitalists, and Henry wrote wildly, "I want to put every money-lender to death. . . . In the coming rows, you will know where to find me. Probably I shall be helping the London mob pull Harcourt and Rothschild on a lamp-post in Piccadilly."[12]

Henry Adams had clearly ceased to be a Mugwump. Since his wife, Marian, had committed suicide in 1885, Henry's friends were not Mugwumps but Republicans. His best friend, John Hay, had only contempt for Mugwumps. And his closest woman friend, Elizabeth Cameron, was married to the Republican senator from Pennsylvania. In fact, Senator Don Cameron persuaded Henry of the merits of silver currency. A product of the traditional Pennsylvania industrialist support for protection and

11. "Boston Bimetallism," *New York Times*, Feb. 28, 1894, 4; "International Bimetallism," *Harper's Weekly* 39 (May 12, 1894): 435.
12. Adams to Elizabeth Cameron, Sept. 15, 1893, Adams to Charles Milnes Gaskell, Jan. 23, 1894, in Levenson et al., *Letters of Henry Adams*, 4:128, 156–57; Ernest Samuels, *Henry Adams: The Major Phase*, 118–23; Adams, *Education of Henry Adams*, 334–37.

inflation, Cameron supported silver in the 1890s even after his party became the gold party. Henry credited the Senator with converting him to silver and his brother Brooks with persuading him of the scientific law for banker destruction of producers and civilizations. Henry had abandoned the liberal belief that the commercial world operated as a harmony of interests. In despair, he rejected the liberalism of Mugwumpery. "When I think of the formulas of our youth," he wrote, "when I look at my old set of John Stuart Mill, and suddenly recall that I am actually a member of the Cobden Club, I feel that somewhere there is the biggest kind of joke."[13]

When an Adams who had invested $20,000 in the *New York Evening Post* lost faith in traditional political economy and ceased to be a Mugwump, when "professed teachers of political economy needed to be retaught," American seemed to be collapsing into anarchism. E. L. Godkin feared chaos had won. As Coxey's Army marched on Washington demanding greenbacks, populists screamed for free coinage of silver, and followers of Eugene Debs rioted against government troops in Chicago, Godkin exploded in denunciation of socialist and paternalistic thinking resulting from a generation of tariff protection and from the teachings of new-school economists and social gospel ministers who encouraged the poor to think they too were entitled to special benefits. "Coxeyism has been produced by thirty years of protectionism" Godkin insisted. "The workingmen of America have been taught in eight Presidential canvasses that their wages depend on their vote, that their prosperity depended on legislation to raise prices." For forty years the Republican party had taught that the government should see that workingmen received good wages. Armies now marched to Washington because of the belief that "Congress can make money. . . . This is what greenbackism and silverism and Populism and Coxeyism mean." Godkin concluded, "protectionism leads straight to socialism, of which Coxeyism is simply a filthy eruption."[14]

Godkin represented eastern urbanites, who viewed the poor not as nice people but low white crackers from southern farms who had always hated civilization and upper classes. His poor were also the immigrant

13. Adams, *Education of Henry Adams,* 334–35; Brooks Adams, "The Heritage of Henry Adams," introduction to Henry Adams, *The Degradation of the Democratic Dogma* (New York: Macmillan, 1919), 90–96; Adams to Gaskell, Sept. 27, 1894, in Levenson et al., *Letters of Henry Adams,* 4:215.
14. E. L. Godkin, "Who Is Responsible for Coxey?" "The Republican Tweedledum and the Democratic Tweedledee," *Nation* 58 (May 3, 1894): 323–24.

working class with "half-civilized foreigners drawn from the lowest races of Europe, who live in a state of savage and chronic discontent. . . ." These poor had been encouraged in their crazes, Godkin said, by men of education. "The silver craze has been helped along by the bimetallists, professors and instructed cranks. They kept telling the silverites that they were right in principle," Godkin said. "The labor craze," he added, "fanned and promoted by 'ethical' professors and clergymen ended in the Chicago riots. . . ." Godkin feared that "thousands of weak brains in both Europe and America are waiting today to have their murderous passions lighted by a word or two in favor of 'social evolution' by some light-headed professor or half-baked minister who has been overcome by the spectacle of human misery." "As the world now stands," Godkin wrote, "we hold it to be the solemn duty of all writers, preachers, professors, who are engaged in the work of reform, to refrain from denunciations of the existing society and social arrangement."[15]

The old, bitter, nearly retired Godkin may have given up hope that education could establish a virtuous community. His hatred of new-school professors did not drive him to engage in academic purges. He resisted telling the Johns Hopkins president that "Professors of Political Economy preaching their own philanthropic gospel as 'Science,' are among the most dangerous characters of our time, and Ely was one of them," until Professor Ely had resigned for a Wisconsin position. Godkin did encourage a critical Wisconsin letter to be published in the *Nation* in the summer of 1894, and the resulting University of Wisconsin heresy trial forced Ely into quiet conformity in order to hold his job.[16]

While Godkin concentrated his bitter invective on radical professors, populists, and protectionists, his more sober associate editor, Horace White, developed a message that the greenbacks must go. According to White, the Legal Tender Act of the Civil War had "taught people to believe lies . . . that the Government could make money." In asserting that only gold could be money, White was saying that governments should not make paper and silver money because political temptations always led to corruption. The only way to avoid currency scandal, White argued in the *Nation*

15. E. L. Godkin, "What It Has All Come To," *Nation* 58 (June 21, 1894): 463; "Causes of the Present Discontent," *Springfield Republican,* June 30, 1894, 4; Godkin to Charles Eliot Norton, July 13, 1896, Charles Eliot Norton Papers, Houghton Library, Harvard.

16. Godkin to Daniel Coit Gilman, Feb. 17, 1892, in Armstrong, *Gilded Age Letters of E. L. Godkin,* 432; Rader, *Academic Mind,* 136–58.

and in his book *Money and Banking* (1895), was to get the government out of the banking business and turn money over to the banks.[17]

The *Nation* editors entered the presidential campaign year of 1896 agreeing with other Mugwump journals—the *New York Times, Harper's Weekly, Boston Herald,* and *Springfield Republican*—that Congress and the Republican party represented the enemy. Only Democratic president Grover Cleveland had saved the gold standard with his silver repeal and his bond issues to preserve the gold reserve. Republican protectionists had continued to be supportive of silver, and the Republican presidential front-runner, William McKinley, was said to be no better than James G. Blaine. The *New York Times* declared early against McKinley, declaring; "His protectionism is too extreme and foolish. His views on the currency are too vague and risky." The trouble with McKinley was that he had been on all sides of the silver question, voting for and against free silver. The *Times* concluded that he had "no convictions whatever as to whether the gold standard or the silver standard or a double standard would be best for the business of the country . . . his speeches on the subject are pure demagoguery. They betray an anxious desire to say what he thinks will be most acceptable; they are full of catch-words and vague phrases and pompous generalities."[18]

Character in a president seemed essential to Mugwumps because they had no trust in Congress. As Godkin explained, "Congress and the Legislatures are going rapidly down hill, and are likely to be worse before they are better. They are clearly incompetent to govern a great commercial country, and we must rely . . . on putting vigorous men of known character and opinions in the Presidential chair, not to legislate, but to prevent mischief." McKinley could not be the Mugwump executive because his notoriously weak character had been exposed by his support of both sides of the free silver coinage debate. Nomination and election of the weak McKinley, Godkin predicted, "will cause one of the greatest panics in modern history."[19]

Mugwumps never developed affection for McKinley but came to regard him as a lesser evil when silverites captured the Democratic party,

17. Horace White, "The Greenbacks Must Go," *Nation* 59 (Dec. 13, 1894): 438; Horace White, *Money and Banking* (Boston: Ginn, 1895).

18. "The Republican Convention," *New York Times,* Mar. 24, 1896, 4; "The Political Situation," *New York Times,* Apr. 20, 1896, 4.

19. E. L. Godkin, "A Word to Business Men," "Platforms," *Nation* 62 (May 14, May 28, 1896): 371–72, 410.

repudiated President Cleveland, wrote free silver platforms, and nominated William Jennings Bryan for the presidency. Mugwumps immediately shifted from criticizing McKinley to stopping Bryan. The fighting words *greed, prejudice, envy,* and *theft* studded Mugwump accusations of Bryan's goal to take half the savings of the frugal by making all obligations payable in silver dollars worth 53 cents in gold. Horace White of the *Nation* declared: "The time has come for every man who has saved anything, even though it be only ten dollars in a savings bank, to fight for the ownership of it. The demand for a free-coinage is a demand for a division of property." Bryan, Mugwumps determined, "must be crushed."[20]

Historians have criticized Mugwumps for using misleading moralistic rhetoric—"the honest dollar"—rather than examining the actual justice that might result from a stable managed currency. To be sure, Mugwumps thought "virtue" and "honesty" were precisely what elections ought to be about and would never have found any congressionally managed currency unacceptable. While admitting that prices had declined, they insisted that falling prices were no simple response to currency contraction. Prices had declined even as the Treasury Department expanded the money supply with purchases of millions in silver. Nine varieties of American currency had also been expanded by bank deposits and personal checks, which surely acted just like money. And prices had not fallen solely because of the money supply; the falling price of wheat resulted more from the competition of new wheat production in Australia than from the declining quantity of money. Growth in productivity and efficiency were very much a part of the price decline. In short, Mugwumps popularized the findings of professor J. Laurence Laughlin's Harvard graduate students, who researched limitations of the quantity theory of money in an effort to undermine the silver case for expanding the money supply.[21]

Classical economists believed that very few of the hardships of American life required action from the government. Troubles and suffering of farmers resulted from overproduction that did not justify "dishonesty" or the creation of a paternalistic government, which would "mean the plunging of the United States into an age so dark that the imagination

20. Horace White, "The Issue of the Campaign," *Nation* 63 (July 2, 1896): 4.

21. "Some Populist Fallacies," *Harper's Weekly* 40 (July 11, 1896): 674; "Dealing with Delusion," *New York Times*, July 16, 1896, 4; Alfred Bornemann, *J. Laurence Laughlin* (Washington: American Council on Public Affairs, 1940), 44.

shudders at the prospect of such a reign of brutal and besotted ignorance as the civilized world has not known for centuries."[22]

Had Mugwumps been purely self-interested supporters of creditor interests, they could have rallied around McKinley and his Republican party, which firmly endorsed the gold standard for the campaign of 1896. But Mugwumps remained troubled by his tariff and his lack of commitment to free-market principles. By defeating Bryan they were helping McKinley win, but many did not wish to vote for him. Independent principles were best preserved by supporting a splinter party in 1896. Mugwumps encouraged Cleveland Democrats to assemble in Indianapolis and nominate Illinois Senator John M. Palmer, a Democrat sound on currency and the tariff, as their candidate. And so the National Democratic party or "Gold Democrats" as they were known, organized to support principle and not party, just as the Free-Soil party had done.[23]

The National Democratic party offered a forum for old Mugwumps such as Edward Atkinson to write and dispense educational propaganda. "My time is devoted entirely to the defeat of the silver cranks," he happily reported. He could not understand a dropout such as Charles Francis Adams Jr., who said he let himself be " 'rounded up' into McKinleyism as infinitely the less of two evils. . . ." No Mugwump could say, as Adams did: "I have given up all discussion of matters now in agitation. I have come to the conclusion that 'life is a failure.' " To lose faith in liberal education and the value of preserving a balance of power between the two parties, as Adams had, meant a desertion of Mugwumpery.[24]

In the November vote, only 132,000 Americans actually cast their ballots for the Gold Democrat John M. Palmer. Some Mugwumps had voted for McKinley to make certain Bryan never won. The McKinley victory prevented inflation from winning in 1896 but never promised victory for the Mugwump principle of limited government. McKinley Republicans were the big-government party and could not be trusted with political management of the currency. Horace White and Charles Dunbar insisted on taking up the money question at the end of the campaign.

22. "The Triumph of Sectionalism and Communism," *Harper's Weekly* 40 (July 18, 1896): 698.

23. Blodgett, *Gentle Reformers*, 224–28; "The Third Ticket," *New York Times*, Aug. 26, 1896, 4; Fleming, *R. R. Bowker*, 266–70.

24. Fleming, *R. R. Bowker*, 268–70; Atkinson to Edward Oldham, Charles Francis Adams to Atkinson, Sept. 24, 1896, Atkinson Papers.

"The fight we have just passed through will be renewed," White warned. "There can be no peace until the Government is taken out of the banking business. All forms of Government demand-notes and circulating paper must be retired. To make the victory . . . lasting, something must be done to make the currency automatic." Mugwumps continued to push banking reform on banks, businessmen, and politicians, but few would live to see Woodrow Wilson finally enact their reform.[25]

---

25. Horace White, "Currency Reform," *Nation* 63 (Nov. 12, 1896): 358; Charles F. Dunbar, "The Safety of the Legal Tender Paper," *Quarterly Journal of Economics* 11 (Apr. 1897): 236–43; for the creation of the Federal Reserve, see James Livingston, *Origins of the Federal Reserve System: Money, Class, and Corporate Capitalism*.

10

Anti-imperialism

The world's best escape from the ancient folly of militarism and imperialism had been America. A new land with a thin population and weak neighbors, free of the burden of supporting a standing army or a large regulatory government, could follow George Washington in the tradition of avoiding foreign wars. A republic of peace and prosperity became the normal condition for Americans. When free to pursue their goals, individuals demonstrated industry, frugality, and domestic happiness, and persuaded the visiting Alexis de Tocqueville that Americans were the freest and most enlightened people placed in the happiest condition in the world. Their most conspicuous lapses from pacifism—the Mexican War and the Civil War—were excused as evils of the Southern slave power. But liberals were not absolute pacifists; they, like John Stuart Mill, applauded war if it were for a moral purpose such as extending liberty to African Americans. When America quickly demobilized after the Civil War to a standing army of only 25,000, Mugwumps continued to recommend their country as the role model for European nations cursed by "enormous military establishments" of four million men. The American republic stood as the world's best model of a land where "security and prosperity" were possible without soldiers.[1]

The connection of pacifism and liberalism had been spelled out by Richard Cobden. The Manchester manufacturer's first pamphlet, *England, Ireland, and America* (1835) had opposed war and armed interventions in the foreign policy of Britain. Armed conflict bled peoples of men and money, Cobden complained, destroying trade, employment, and resources. War impoverished a people, leaving them with destruction,

1. E. L. Godkin, "What the United States Do for Europe," *Nation* 32 (Jan. 6, 1881): 4–5; Atkinson, *Industrial Progress of the Nation*, 67–71.

economic depression, and a burden of debt. If all the millions spent for armaments were instead thrown into the sea, the people would be better off. To liberate individuals from suffering, Cobden urged the British government to stop armed interventions and mercantilistic regulations of trade. While war and regulations destroyed, Cobden said, peace and liberty created prosperity. Cobden sought a shift in British foreign policy from aggression to a peaceful policy like that of the United States. "It is to the industry, the economy, and peaceful policy of America," Cobden warned, "that the power and greatness of England are in danger of being superseded, yes, by the successful rivalry of America shall we, in all probability, be placed second in the rank of nations."[2]

America provided Cobden a favorite illustration for teaching peace and free trade as the path to prosperity and happiness. Other governments created misery in the world, but in America, individuals and trade were left alone to prosper and flourish. To promote freedom and prosperity in other nations, Cobden attended peace conferences, talking international disarmament, arbitration, and free trade. Free markets removed barriers separating peoples, permitting them to experience the world market as mutual gain rather than a war of interests. Government intervention in markets and in the affairs of other countries only produced grief; government intervention increased suffering. Cobden insisted that imperialism, colonies, and protection were a delusion, creating not wealth but financial burdens. For Cobdenites, free trade and the peace movement were "one and the same cause" for mutual gain and no exploitation.[3]

American liberals consistently opposed territorial expansion, which deprived others of freedom and exploited them for the benefit of colonizers. Bayonets and colonies were the road back to Old World troubles rather than a future of progress and prosperity; freer markets were the peaceful and mutually beneficial road pointed out by Adam Smith, Richard Cobden, and John Stuart Mill. Mugwumps felt compelled to denounce President Grant's annexation plans for Santo Domingo in 1869, just as they stood against Republican imperialist plans for building a great navy and annexing Caribbean and Hawaiian islands in the 1890s.[4]

2. William H. Dawson, *Richard Cobden and Foreign Policy*, 93–94, 131–32, 231; Wendy Hinde, *Richard Cobden: A Victorian Outsider*, 16–20, 202–9.
3. Dawson, *Richard Cobden and Foreign Policy*, 93–94, 118–19, 131–32, 231; Hinde, *Richard Cobden*, 16–20, 207–9.
4. William S. McFeely, *Grant* (New York: Norton, 1982), 337–52; E. L. Godkin, "The Annexation Fever," *Nation* 8 (Apr. 15, 1869): 289; Robert L. Beisner, "Thirty Years before

The new imperialism organized around the writings of U.S. Navy captain Alfred Thayer Mahan, who argued that America needed a modern navy and refueling bases around the world in order to become a world power. Specifically, America needed Hawaii and probably Cuba, according to Mahan. E. L. Godkin objected, maintaining that navalists and military men ought never be permitted to make national policy. Captain Mahan and the large-navy advocates did not want a powerful fleet just for defense but "to fight somebody." Big-navy Republicans had exhibited the hostility to foreigners, thirst for glory, and a readiness for war that made Godkin fear for the future. A large navy would only lead to war. "We cannot be invaded, we have no foreign possessions to lose," so a small navy for coastal defense was more than adequate, unless America planned to start a war, the *Nation* insisted.[5]

Godkin expressed the old liberal concern for individual liberty that made him distrustful of governments. But a new generation educated in the 1870s and 1880s learned a nationalism schooled by German unification under Bismarck and the British conquest of Africa. All the great European states deserted liberalism to acquire colonies and expand government powers. New Darwinian notions gave "scientific" sanction to war, racism, and the domination of "lesser" cultures. In the struggle for survival, the new generation epitomized by Theodore Roosevelt did not want America to go soft and weak or their government to remain small and limited. "If we come to nothing as a nation," Roosevelt wrote Lodge in 1896, "it will be because of the teaching of Carl Schurz, President Eliot, the *Evening Post* and the futile sentimentalists of the international arbitration type, bears its legitimate fruit in producing a flabby, timid type of character, which eats away the great fighting features of our race."[6]

Roosevelt fretted more about his manhood than his virtue, demonstrating the truth of conventional wisdom that once a Mugwump entered politics he ceased to be a Mugwump. Obsessed with preserving American masculinity, Roosevelt replaced Mugwump peace and justice with Social

Manila: E. L. Godkin, Carl Schurz, and Anti-imperialism in the Gilded Age," *Historian* 30 (Aug. 1968): 561–77.

5. E. L. Godkin, "Naval Politics," *Nation* 56 (Mar. 9, 1893): 173–74; "Armed Evangelists," *Nation* 56 (Mar. 16, 1893): 190–91.

6. For the new diplomacy, see Robert L. Beisner, *From the Old Diplomacy to the New, 1865–1900* (New York: Crowell, 1975), 73–76; Theodore Roosevelt to Henry Cabot Lodge, Apr. 29, 1896, in Morison, Blum, and Buckley, *Letters of Theodore Roosevelt,* 1:535–36; Charles W. Eliot was Harvard's Mugwump president.

Darwinian courage, bravery, and violence. Manliness must be asserted by making war and exercising what he called "the great fighting, masterful virtues. . . ." While Mugwump Christians refused to deprive others of life, liberty, or property, Darwinian Republicans could not wait to take from other peoples and prove the supremacy of American Anglo-Saxons.

Republican plans to annex the Hawaiian Islands in 1893 were dashed when Grover Cleveland returned to the White House. A disappointed Senator Henry Cabot Lodge took his frustration out on Mugwumps, accusing them of having abused the navy, sneered at Americanism, and "Cobdenized the Democratic party." Lodge wanted an imperialistic foreign policy to annex the Hawaiian Islands as well as Cuba and Canada, which he justified as in step with modern trends, good for the economy, and good for "the pride of country and of race." The trouble with the tariff reformers, he complained, was that they acted on the Manchester school theory that "armies, navies, war, territorial extension, or national expansion must be stopped because they were likely to interfere with the complete freedom of trade." The old Democratic party of Jefferson, Jackson, and Polk had a record of "conquest, colonization, and territorial expansion unequalled by any people in the nineteenth century," Lodge pointed out, but the disciples of Cobden had taken over the Democratic party and ruined American foreign policy by the assumption that peace was more important than "a nation's honor" or "the advance of a race."[7]

Republican jingoism of pride and aggression proved so popular that President Cleveland pandered to his expansionist critics by taking up their militancy and threatening war with Great Britain if that nation did not accept American settlement of the Venezuelan boundary dispute. Shocked Mugwumps blasted President Cleveland for his jingoistic message. Charles Eliot Norton saw the "astounding" message as confirmation of fears that moral character had so declined as to endanger American civilization. With ambitious Washington politicians disparaging the virtues of peace and goodwill, advocating war and aggression, the nation was in danger of deserting its liberal tradition.[8]

Mugwumps feared that the national character had changed. No longer did Americans insist on peaceful development and no exploitation of

7. Henry Cabot Lodge, "Our Blundering Foreign Policy," *Forum* 19 (Mar. 1895): 13–15, 17.

8. Godkin to Charles Eliot Norton, Dec. 29, 1895, Godkin to James Bryce, Jan. 9, 1896, in Armstrong, *Gilded Age Letters of E. L. Godkin,* 475, 477; Charles Eliot Norton, "Some Aspects of Civilization in America," *Forum* 20 (Feb. 1896): 469, 651.

others. The cheap press had taught, Godkin said, that America ought to use force to gratify desires and ambitions. And the newly elected President William McKinley could not restrain the imperialists in his party or those in the daily newspapers. A politician in step with the yellow journalism of jingoism, Henry Cabot Lodge's friend Theodore Roosevelt, in his first public address as the Assistant Secretary of the Navy, repeated the word "war" sixty-two times. Roosevelt wanted a good war to encourage martial virtues in young Americans. And he had only scorn and disgust for the conservative McKinley-Hanna alliance of business and politics, which feared war. "No triumph of peace is quite so great as the supreme triumphs of war," Roosevelt told the Naval War College.[9]

So offensive was the imperialism of Roosevelt and Lodge to Mugwumps that they would have been surprised to know that foreign policy scholars two generations later were suggesting that anti-imperialists had differed little from imperialists. Professor William A. Williams abolished the differences by throwing his net for expansionists so wide that it pulled in all who believed America needed foreign markets. If the origin of imperialism lay in capitalist markets, then Mugwumps, who certainly believed in peaceful trade, were declared to differ from Mahan, Lodge, and Roosevelt only "in degree, not in kind."[10]

The Williams thesis would have been considered nonsense by any Cobdenite who had spent a lifetime opposing colonialism. The central fact of trade for liberals was that it should be a free market for individuals to pursue mutual gain. Governments should have no role in that trade; laissez-faire meant no tariffs, no bayonets, and no colonies.[11] America had started down the path to colonialism, Mugwumps thought, when the Civil War Congress began to impose protective tariffs and expand the money supply. A new mercantilism had grown up with Republicans preaching paternalistic government interventions to support selfish trade and commerce. By the nineties, Republicans were calling for government to start wars to revive business and pull the nation out of economic depression.

9. E. L. Godkin, "The Education of War," *Nation* 66 (Apr. 21, 1898): 296–97; Edmund Morris, *The Rise of Theodore Roosevelt*, 424, 569–71, 583.

10. William A. Williams, *The Tragedy of American Diplomacy* (New York: Dell, 1962), 38; Walter Lafeber, *The New Empire: An Interpretation of American Expansion, 1860–1898*, 416.

11. Logsdon, *Horace White*, 357–60; E. L. Godkin, "Americanism," *Nation* 56 (Feb. 23, 1893): 136–37.

For Godkin, Norton, or any other Mugwump, war between nations represented a relic of barbarism that repudiated liberal civilization. To be sure, war for a moral reason, such as eliminating slavery, might be necessary. But to kill for trade seemed even lower than the savages of barbaric times. When the economic arguments for war were advocated by the *Detroit Tribune* and by Nebraska Senator J. M. Thurston, Godkin declared these "open avowals of readiness to kill people and destroy property for private gain . . . the most grotesque outcome of Christianity and civilization. . . ." War amounted to robbery and murder, and "to fight for the sake of fighting, and above all to fight in order to make business lively," he said, "sinks civilized man below the savage."[12]

Mugwumps were social evolutionists who knew civilization evolved, but they were definitely not Social Darwinists willing to believe competition among races must be fought out on the battlefield. The doctrine of evolution no more justified annexation of distant lands to them than did the Calvinist doctrine of predestination. Professor William Graham Sumner, who taught Darwinism at Yale, knew human values changed over time, but he absolutely refused to regard liberal values as relative. He was a Cobdenite who knew imperialism to be a disastrous relic of the Old World. America had emerged in rebellion against that Old World folly of empire, foreign domination, and imperialism. If additional evidence were needed for the economic disaster of imperialism, Sumner explained the economic history of Spain. Spanish power had dominated the world in the 1500s, but imperialism proved her ruin; Spain declined from the greatest to the least power. Power and wealth did not flow from annexation, Sumner insisted, but from free peoples and free markets where industry, frugality, and prudence were honored. Imperialism and militarism diverted people from their own interests and consumed the products of their science, art, industry, and savings. Sumner might be a Darwinist, but he was also a Cobdenite who had no trouble preaching the folly of imperialism and the wisdom of preserving American character, principles, and institutions, including the Declaration of Independence and the Constitution.[13]

12. E. L. Godkin, "The War in Its Right Place," *Nation* 66 (Mar. 31, 1898): 238.
13. William Graham Sumner, "The Fallacy of Territorial Extension," (1896), "The Conquest of the United States by Spain," (1898), and "War," (1903), reprinted in *War and Other Essays* (New Haven: Yale University Press, 1911), 285–92, 297, 307–10, 325–27; Richard Hofstadter, *Social Darwinism in American Thought* (Boston: Beacon, 1955), 64, 195.

It is a revisionist misunderstanding to think Sumner and other Mug-wumps were racists who did not really believe in the Declaration of Independence. This great document of western liberalism let individuals create their own government for the protection of their life, liberty, and property. Freedom and natural rights were core Mugwump beliefs, along with the benevolent ethic that neither individuals nor nations should exploit others. Mugwumps were anti-imperialists because they were liberals, republicans, and moralists. To insist that racism motivated their anti-imperialism is to get Mugwump priorities wrong. Their liberal, Cobdenite principles rejected annexation. To be sure, they were not believers in equality of abilities, but neither were Abraham Lincoln and Thomas Jefferson. Jeffersonian equality had been one of equal political rights but not individual abilities, and this was the Mugwump case against imperialism; inhabitants had a right to govern themselves, and whether they established "good government" was not America's affair.[14]

Mugwumps believed education, character, and the free market were more important than race. Edward Atkinson, although he bitterly opposed imperialism on principle, clearly believed free markets could Americanize tropical natives. He privately assured his friend David A. Wells that the annexation of Cuba could be as successful as that of Texas or Alaska. The key to progress for Atkinson was the free-market system: Cuba would be Americanized by the incentive of profit. Carl Schurz did not share the optimism about tropical peoples. He that feared climate, race, and culture were stronger forces than those that might lead to Americanization. Schurz is usually the Mugwump cited to support the thesis that racism was the dark force opposing expansion. But race was never Schurz's main argument against imperialism, and he was certainly no Darwinian racist. He continued to be an advocate of equality for African Americans, opposing silly segregation and disfranchisement.[15]

14. Christopher Lasch labeled the Mugwumps racist in his first article, "The Anti-imperialists, the Philippines, and the Inequality of Man," reprinted in *The World of Nations* (New York: Vintage, 1974), 70–79; for a test of the evidence, see Richard E. Welch Jr., "Motives and Policy Objectives of Anti-imperialists, 1898," *Mid-America* 51 (Apr. 1969): 119–29; and a rejection of the Lasch "nonsense," James M. McPherson, *The Abolitionist Legacy: From Reconstruction to the NAACP* (Princeton: Princeton University Press, 1975), 326–31. E. L. Godkin, "What to Do With the Philippines," *Nation* 67 (Oct. 6, 1898): 253–54.

15. Atkinson to Wells, July 8, 1898, reel 7, 4338, Wells Papers; for Schurz's defense of African Americans, see Frederic Bancroft, ed., *Speeches, Correspondence, and Political Papers of Carl Schurz* (New York: G. P. Putnam's, 1913), "Can the South Solve the Negro Problem?" 6:311–48; for his alien race argument, see pp. 12–14.

Mugwump illusions that America could be different from Europe were shattered when President McKinley capitulated to the popular demand for liberating Cuba and forced Spain to declare war. "The old America, the America of our hopes and our dreams has come to an end," Charles Eliot Norton wrote, "and a new America is entering on the false course which has been tried so often. . . ." E. L. Godkin agreed, "I too tremble at the thought of having a large navy and the war making power, lodged in the hands of such puerile and thoughtless people—100,000,000 strong. It is an awful prospect for the world, and I am glad to be so near the end of my career." Godkin had come to the United States fifty years before with high hopes, but now those liberal illusions were shattered. "American ideals were the intellectual food of my youth," he said, "and to see America converted into a senseless, old world conqueror, embitters my age." The bitter Godkin was unable to continue as editor of the *Nation.* In 1899 the disillusioned old liberal threw in the towel and retired in England.[16]

Other Mugwumps refused to quit. Carl Schurz, an energetic sixty-nine-year-old, urged President McKinley to prevent the Spanish-American War from becoming a grab for empire. McKinley must adhere to his original humanitarian war declaration, resist annexing any colony, and remember that he had earlier declared annexation by force to be "criminal aggression." In addition to keeping his word by ending the imperialistic talk, McKinley would be preserving the republican institutions of America, which rested on a belief in liberty and self-determination of peoples. The honorable course would also be the best national commercial policy, giving America greater trade without the cost of standing armies, navies, and wars. While Schurz is usually quoted as the racist Mugwump who objected to imperialism because of his contempt for natives, he made no argument of race in his letters to McKinley. Only later did Schurz add to public speeches that tropical peoples had never governed themselves by democracy. Schurz warned that if America went on an imperialistic run, adding perhaps fifteen new states and thirty senators from peoples whose languages and culture were Spanish creole, Negro, Malay, and Tagal, the American political system would be corrupted and Spanish Americans would select our presidents. America was a racist country and perhaps Schurz used the racist argument to gain support for anti-imperialism.

16. Norton to Edward Le-Child, June 26, 1898, in Norton and Howe, *Letters of Charles Eliot Norton,* 2:272–73; Godkin to Norton, Nov. 29, 1899, in Armstrong, *Gilded Age Letters of E. L. Godkin,* 515, 521.

But race was only a brief and minor Schurz theme. His major permanent themes were moral, republican, and Cobdenite.[17]

Boston Mugwumps assembled in Faneuil Hall on June 15, 1898, the day a congressional resolution annexed Hawaii. Gamaliel Bradford, retired banker and *Nation* essayist, called the meeting to ask that liberals oppose not the Spanish-American War but Congress's betrayal of the original humanitarian intent. The Congress, which had originally declared solely for Cuban independence, now talked of empire. "The politicians and the editors who clamored for humanity now shriek for empire," Bradford declared. Politicians clamored for "Puerto Rico, the Philippine Islands, the Ladrones, the Canaries and every other colony of Spain to our territories, and to embark this country in a career of foreign conquest. It is even suggested that we seize the Hawaiian Islands."[18]

Bradford organized the public meeting because a great republican principle was threatened. For more than a hundred years, the American government had rested on the principle that governments derive their just powers from the consent of the governed. Seizing any colony of Spain violated the republican principle as well as the great biblical commandment against theft. While Spanish natives might be unfit for self-government, Americans could not decide that issue. The fundamental principle of the founding fathers had been that "all men are equal before the law and have equal political rights." If the wise policy of nonintervention in other people's affairs were disregarded, Americans would suffer at home from increasingly oppressive taxation and corruption in government. "Imperialism abroad will bring imperialism at home," Bradford warned. America would go the way of the Roman republic if it broke with moral principles. "When Rome began her career of conquest, the Roman republic began to decay."[19]

The Boston meeting resolved to organize committees of correspondence to extend their network of concerned public moralists throughout the country. And on November 19, 1898, their Anti-Imperialist League officially organized. While the league would claim members in 45 states, the battle over imperialism waged mainly in the East between generations, seventy-year-old Mugwumps versus forty-year-old imperialists. To be sure, Mugwumps sought to broaden their appeal by inviting in a few

---

17. Bancroft, *Speeches, Correspondence, and Political Papers of Carl Schurz,* 5:465–66, 472, 473, 475, 478–89, 494–510; 6:8–36, 77–120.

18. *Boston Evening Transcript,* June 15, 1898, p. 9.

19. Ibid.

old professional Republican politicians, George S. Boutwell and John Sherman, and Democrats Grover Cleveland and Richard Olney, as well as the steel capitalist Andrew Carnegie. The League represented a coalition of elderly leadership.[20]

The Anti-Imperialist League presented the last act of the Mugwump drama. Some were dying—David A. Wells died in 1898—and most of the others would be gone within a decade. Their time had passed. They were the Civil War moralists who talked of personal liberty and no exploitation, while the new generation shouted for national conquest and dominance. They were told by the rude young imperialists that this war, and the public leadership, now belonged to a new generation.

Nineteenth-century public moralists were expected to give way to twentieth-century leaders. Men educated in a moral philosophy that said that God had created the world to be run by classical liberalism were asked to step aside for younger public moralists, who knew God created a Social Darwinian world where peoples had to be ruled by the superior empires. The Cobdenite golden rule in foreign policy was to be replaced by Bismarck's blood and iron. Civilized states were destined to colonize barbarians for naval bases, raw materials, markets, and prestige, as well as proper Christianizing and uplifting. The teachings in the colleges and churches had changed. Of all the Christian denominations in America, only the tiny Quakers and Unitarians objected to the new American imperialism. Positive government had become the new wisdom. All the European states had deserted Cobden for the new imperialism, with Great Britain leading the work by adding more than four million square miles of territory to her empire.[21] America must get in step; the old liberalism of individual freedom had to go.

While expansionists indulged Americans to revel in nationalistic glory, Mugwumps offered only moral restraint. Expansionists promised sharing the pleasures of foreign conquest—a future of jobs, riches, national security, and pride—but Mugwumps offered only self-denial and faithfulness to past principles. America must not imitate Old World nations, the Mugwumps insisted, because expansion ran counter to the principle of

20. E. Berkeley Tompkins, *Anti-imperialism in the United States: The Great Debate, 1890–1920*, 158–59.

21. David Healy, *U.S. Expansionism: The Imperialist Urge in the 1890s* (Madison: University of Wisconsin Press, 1970), 11–21; Julius W. Pratt, *The Expansionists of 1898* (Baltimore: Johns Hopkins Press, 1936), 288–89; Beisner, *From the Old Diplomacy to the New*, 72–81.

the Declaration of Independence, Washington's Farewell Address, and Lincoln's Gettysburg Address—a government could not rule peoples without their consent.

To preserve their traditional American republic, Mugwumps produced a blizzard of pamphlets, articles, and speeches, organizing the moral forces of the country to lobby President and Senate against accepting the treaty with Spain, which ceded Puerto Rico, the Philippines, and Guam. The Constitution required a two-thirds majority for ratification of a treaty, and Mugwumps hoped to defeat the Spanish treaty. In the Senate vote, two Republicans joined 25 Democrats in opposing the annexation treaty, falling two votes short of blocking annexation on February 6, 1899. Mugwumps believed they would have won if William Jennings Bryan had not urged Democratic Senators to vote for ratification, advice that anti-imperialists could understand only as a politician's perverse scheme to keep imperialism a burning issue to run against in the presidential election of 1900. While Bryan claimed to be anti-imperialist, no Mugwump thought him anything more than a shifty politician.[22]

Filipinos rebelled for independence in February 1899, keeping the American betrayal of the Declaration of Independence on the front page of American newspapers. The brutalities of guerrilla war offered the opportunity for seventy-one-year-old Edward Atkinson to achieve prominence as a leading anti-imperialist. Atkinson offered his antiwar pamphlets, "The Cost of a National Crime," "The Hell of War and Its Penalties," and "Criminal Aggression: By Whom Committed," to the Secretary of War and announced his intentions of sending the pamphlets to U.S. soldiers in the Philippines. To be sure, the Postmaster General ordered all Atkinson pamphlets to be searched out and removed before the mails were shipped out to the Philippines. This government censorship served to advertise the Atkinson pamphlets and brought Atkinson fame. The Boston Mugwump was certainly one of those anti-imperialists who Theodore Roosevelt declared were "lunatics," "vermin," and unhung "traitors to the country."[23]

The anti-imperialist speeches of Carl Schurz were equally unpatriotic to the ear of a war defender. Schurz portrayed Filipinos and their leader

22. Fred H. Harrington, "The Anti-imperialist Movement in the United States, 1898–1900"; Richard E. Welch Jr., *George Frisbie Hoar and the Half-Breed Republicans* (Cambridge: Harvard University Press, 1971), 229–44.

23. Richard E. Welch, *Response to Imperialism: The United States and the Philippine-American War*, 45–51; Morison, Blum, and Buckley, *Letters of Theodore Roosevelt*, 2:1356, 1368.

Aguinaldo as freedom fighters standing up to McKinley's monstrous war of "criminal aggression." Schurz praised the "tens of thousands" of "innocents" who were slaughtered by a guilty American government characterized by "deceit, false pretense, brutal treachery." McKinley had betrayed the fundamental principles of democracy, sacrificing five thousand American soldiers in a "wicked," "stupid" war.[24]

The great debate ended badly for Mugwumps in 1900, when they were forced to choose between "dreadful" alternatives, Bryan and McKinley. They generally chose Bryan. As Schurz explained, "if a cruel fate should force me to choose between McKinley and the imperialistic policy, and Bryan as the anti-imperialist candidate, I should consider it my duty—a horrible duty—to swallow my personal disgust to defeat—or, at least, try to defeat—imperialism at any cost." Anti-imperialism won few votes for Bryan except perhaps in Massachusetts, where his vote increased 12 percent.[25] Outside New England, Bryan won fewer votes than in 1896. In rejecting Bryan, the nation endorsed colonialism and the positive welfare state of McKinley and Roosevelt.

The Anti-Imperialist League lived on in Boston, inserting Philippine independence planks in the Democratic platform every four years. In 1916 the league finally secured congressional passage of the Jones Bill, promising self-government to the Philippines. The Mugwump freedom cause, renouncing territorial acquisition, had finally won, but neither they nor their league lived to see Philippine independence. The last man in the league, Moorfield Story, wrote in 1923: "Almost everybody who belonged to it is dead, and the young men do not take up the work. I am still its representative, but I have no followers."[26]

24. Bancroft, *Speeches, Correspondence, and Political Papers of Carl Schurz*, 6:77–120, 150–90, 215–56.
25. Harrington, "Anti-imperialist Movement," 228; Schurz to C. F. Adams Jr., Nov. 5, 1899, in Bancroft, *Speeches, Correspondence, and Political Papers of Carl Schurz*, 6:262.
26. M. A. DeWolfe Howe, *Portrait of an Independent: Moorfield Storey*, 250.

11

Mugwumpery

Senator George F. Hoar sought to compliment Edward Atkinson during the anti-imperialist debates by telling him he was too honest and personable to be a Mugwump. "Whatever you are," Hoar said, "you are not a Mugwump." The professional politician had often felt the sting of liberal criticism and sought to dismiss the public moralists as arrogant and contemptible hypocrites motivated by personal pique. Atkinson refused to permit Mugwump to be used as a derogatory smear. Proud of the name for his associates, Atkinson replied, "I am a Mugwump, according to what I believe to be a true interpretation of that very suggestive word."[1]

Where politicians perceived personal spite, Mugwumps recognized moralists motivated by unselfish virtue. Where politicians valued loyalty to political party, Mugwumps valued commitment to moral principle. For intellectuals born in the 1830s and 1840s, Mugwumpery provided an outlet for education in Victorian morality and scientific progress. Liberal reforms expressed concern for the public interest and social science perceptions of the possibilities of human society. Conformity to discovered laws of political economy promised a harmony of interests, elevation of the welfare of the masses, and an end to political corruption.

The liberalism of the Mugwumps would be rudely dismissed by Senator Hoar and later historians. When Hoar denounced Mugwumps for opposing protective tariffs, he defended his own support of powerful manufacturing interests. When twentieth-century historians dismissed the importance of free trade, they reflected a New Deal perception that governments and not free markets offered solutions for the general welfare. For historians who believed in positive government, the tariff was not

---

1. George F. Hoar to Edward Atkinson, Aug. 11, 1898, Atkinson to Hoar, Aug. 12, 1898, Atkinson Papers; for Hoar's story, see Welch, *George Frisbie Hoar.*

immoral pillage or a violation of social science, just boring and unimportant, at least until the last decade of the twentieth century, when free trade emerged again as a remedy for raising world standards of living. Mugwumps might now receive recognition for pointing out that high tariffs did not guarantee high wages. If only 7 percent of Gilded Age Americans worked in protected industries, public moralists had been right to focus on the welfare of the greater majority of workers and consumers. Liberal principles were also correct in connecting regulations of trade with political corruption, the buying of politicians by manufacturing interests. In opposing protective tariffs, Mugwumps stood up to dominant economic interests and promoted the general welfare.

But, it will be argued, Mugwumps did not oppose the biggest business of their day. Liberals did not endorse national regulation of the railroads, the Interstate Commerce Commission of 1887. Their refusal to endorse regulation has been taken as evidence of their capitalist prejudices, but some scholars concede that Americans suffered more from overregulation than they would ever have suffered from a free market.[2] A generation that has quietly abolished the I.C.C. should find merit in Edward Atkinson's perception that railroad promoter Cornelius Vanderbilt achieved his great fortune by reducing the cost of moving a barrel of flour a thousand miles from $3.45 in 1865 to 68 cents in 1885. The capitalist had helped himself by helping others. Vanderbilt's enormous profits were only "trifling," Atkinson thought, when compared with what he saved others. The marketplace, the liberals taught, always worked better than regulation.[3]

Mugwump liberalism deserves recognition for its defense of the market as well as its creation of a modern money and banking system. Rather than denouncing their creed as "archaic" orthodox liberalism, we might thank them for taking money creation out of the hands of Congress. Who would want politicians printing money? An election or a legislature is not the best arena for questions such as the currency supply or the delivery of justice. Courts and Federal Reserve Districts handle justice and the money supply better than popular elections could. And no group in America did more than Mugwumps to get Congress out of money printing and turn the function over to bankers. From 1865 until 1913, Mugwumps were engaged in educating the country to the wisdom of taking the money supply out of politics.

2. This case has been persuasively made by Albro Martin, *Enterprise Denied: Origins of the Decline of American Railroads* (New York: Columbia University Press, 1971).
3. Williamson, *Edward Atkinson*, 253.

Mugwump support for the free market should never be dismissed as mere self-serving capitalist greed. Edward Atkinson pursued no self-interest when he penned his 250 pamphlets. In fact, he even worked against his business interest. His free-trade agitation brought him into direct conflict with his board of directors for the Boston Manufacturers Mutual Fire Insurance Company. After he prepared a 150-page plan for tariff reform in the fall of 1882, alarmed cotton manufacturers criticized Atkinson for having aided a dangerous cause. The chairman of President Atkinson's salary committee told him he was badly misguided. "A great majority of the members of your company are opposed to your tariff policy," Howard Stockton said. "We do not wish to alienate the wool, iron & timber people . . . we honestly think that your views are wrong and they should not be urged."[4]

Under pressure from criticism of his business associates, Atkinson gave way emotionally, writing his friend David Wells, "I suddenly broke down two or three days since from the work and worry of this thing and the sense of responsibility. Sleepless, nervous and depressed."[5] Under the advice of his physician, he took a European trip and gave up tariff reform. He never abandoned his free-trade beliefs, but he shifted his reform work to the money question, which did not stress his business associates.

Mugwumps participated and suffered in these public causes because they believed benevolence was their duty. They even took pleasure in doing this moral calling. Atkinson talked of retiring from business to spend full time in reform work. Although he had never studied moral philosophy in college, the Boston Unitarian had grown up with Charles Norton, regarded Reverend Theodore Parker as a friend, and picked up the same sense of moral obligation to benefit fellow citizens that could be found in the liberal Protestant culture as well as in Francis Wayland's *Moral Science*. Suffering in "the cause of right" had been taught as a clear Christian duty. When Atkinson lost his belief in God is unclear, but he, like other Mugwumps, made a religion of "mutual service." His sense of self-respect required concern for the welfare of others.[6]

4. Howard Stockton to Atkinson, Mar. 24, 1883, Atkinson Papers.
5. Atkinson to Wells, Jan. 1, 1883, letterbooks, Atkinson Papers.
6. Wayland, *Elements of Moral Science*, 336–41. Edward Atkinson "never felt called upon to join any particular church" but believed "mutual service" the higher law for modern society and Unitarianism; see Atkinson, *Industrial Progress of the Nation*, 387; for benevolence without faith, see also Norton to Goldwin Smith, July 12, 1906, in Norton and Howe, *Letters of Charles Eliot Norton*, 2:363–64.

The virtue of benevolence shared mental space with the Mugwumps' confidence that they intellectually understood the world and industrial change.[7] They mastered historical and statistical material that demonstrated that steam and electricity had multiplied the productivity of workers and would create an abundance if only individuals learned personal virtue and if governments withdrew their market interferences. The liberal paradigm gave Mugwumps an intellectual confidence as unshakable as that of the later positive-state Keynesians. In fact, Mugwumps had the additional assurance that came from living in a smaller America when a handful of intellectuals living in Boston and New York could expect to create a new party or to persuade a major party to enact their liberalism.

These liberals and the later New Deal liberals were separated by different paradigms, rather than any lack of concern for the general welfare of the poor. Mugwumps did charity work for the poor in their own communities. Edward Atkinson chartered the Brookline Savings Bank in 1871 and four years later David A. Wells was elected to the board of Chelsea Savings Bank in Norwich, Connecticut. At a time when commercial banks did not accept small depositors, the poor certainly benefited from the unpaid work of middle-class volunteers who opened savings banks for an afternoon a week, took in deposits, and paid interest by investing the savings in government bonds or real estate loans in order to encourage frugality, thrift, and home ownership. The mortgage payment for homes was usually accumulated by the working class in these benevolent thrift institutions, which were typical of northeast communities in the nineteenth century.[8]

Economic liberalism could be given a human touch by the benevolence of Mugwumps, but they were clearly more focused on preventing abuse by wealth than on its distribution. They were not twentieth-century liberals who had lost faith in the market and sought a government redistribution of wealth. And yet they were less hard-hearted than regular Republicans. They did not try to take bread away from the poor in the depression of the 1870s, as the Harvard-trained Unitarian minister, Reverend William G. Eliot, advocated in St. Louis. Reverend Eliot feared Democrats too much to bolt from the Republican party, and he feared the dangerous tramps

7. Daniel Horowitz rejects the charge that reformers held outmoded ideas and failed to understand industrialization; see his "Genteel Observers: New England Economic Writers and Industrialization."

8. Williamson, *Edward Atkinson*, 55–56; Charles M. Coit to Wells, Sept. 15, 1875, reel 3, 1879, Wells Papers; David M. Tucker, *The Decline of Thrift in America: Our Cultural Shift from Saving to Spending* (New York: Praeger, 1991), 39–53.

and vagrants too much to believe the city's free soup kitchen a good idea. Eliot feared St. Louis charity created paupers faster than they could be fed. He repeatedly insisted that the city mayor require able-bodied paupers to work at half-wages and pay for their soup and lodging.[9]

Distrust of the poor and laboring class characterized Republicans more than Mugwumps. None of the liberals wrote an antiunion novel. John Hay's *The Breadwinners* characterizes the views of his fellow McKinley Republicans rather than liberals.[10] E. L. Godkin certainly did criticize unions after the *Evening Post* printers walked off the job in the middle of the day without providing timely notice and then hindered employment of replacement workers. Godkin still conceded that laborers were not free agents in negotiations with capitalists unless they combined in a trade union. Liberals supported freedom and opposed any elimination of competition whether by organized capital or organized labor.

The Mugwumps were a movement of hope rather than fear. They did not fear to break with the Republican party. They were essentially optimistic about the poor and the immigrants. They believed all peoples responded favorably to liberty, education, and free markets. To be sure, they had many harsh words for Tammany Hall and political corruption, but even E. L. Godkin could say, "As soon as the sense of responsibility comes through the accumulation of property they do very well. The Mayors of both New York and Boston just now are Irish Catholics and are the best that either city had for years. In fact Mayor Grace is the best in forty years, or since universal suffrage was introduced." Mugwumps argued that immigration to America had been a success. "We have taken from Europe the poorest, the most ignorant, the most turbulent of her people," James Russell Lowell said, "and have made them over into good citizens, who have added to our wealth, and who are ready to die in defense of a country and of institutions which they know to be worth dying for."[11] Lowell admitted to distress about "hordes of ignorance and poverty" in the great cities, but neither he nor other Mugwumps proposed immigration restriction. It was Republican politician Henry Cabot Lodge who pushed the immigration restriction bill through Congress in 1896.

9. Eliot to Mayor J. H. Britton, Oct. 13, 1875, newspaper clipping of Eliot to Mayor Henry Overstole, Nov. 13, 1877, Notebooks 9 and 10, p. 43, William G. Eliot Collection, Washington University Archives.

10. Sproat misleads readers by using *The Breadwinners* as evidence of liberal antiunion prejudice in his book, "*The Best Men,*" 219.

11. Godkin to Earl Spencer, Sept. 5, 1886, in Armstrong, *Gilded Age Letters of E. L. Godkin,* 346. James Russell Lowell, *Literary and Political Addresses,* 25.

These were no vindictive elitists. The anti-imperialism debates even catapulted some Mugwumps back into civil rights agitation. Moorfield Storey, the young independent who worked with the Adams brothers in the 1870s, became the first president of the NAACP at the same time he presided over the Anti-Imperialist League. The racism of expansionists had so offended Storey that he told Carl Schurz, "We must, for the sake of negroes and Filipinos both rouse again the anti-slavery feeling." And Schurz responded with a published defense of the civil rights of African Americans in *McClure's Magazine*. And Horace White signed the call for a national conference on racism.[12]

Mugwumpery reflected a benevolent liberalism supportive of individual rights and limited government. This culture of moral concern permitted no personal pursuit of office or political self-interest. If Mugwump intent had been only to establish rule by their crowd, they would have been happy with election victories of Henry Cabot Lodge and Theodore Roosevelt. But Mugwumps were no party of the power-hungry; they were a network of public moralists. When Lodge and Roosevelt deserted the specific shared ideas that united liberals, they ceased to be regarded as Mugwumps. When Henry Adams became a silverite, anti-Semite, and imperialist, he ceased to be a Mugwump and a liberal.

Liberalism was certainly not obsolete in the nineteenth century, although Mugwump faith in moral virtue might have been too optimistic. The conviction that citizens would exercise republican virtue in political affairs, supporting the public interest rather than individual self-interest, retained less than majority support. Manufacturers clearly demonstrated an overpowering concern for self-interest, corrupting the political process in pursuit of tariff protection. If steel producers had their government price supports, then farmers could not have been expected to neglect their self-interest and not organize a People's Party asking for government subsidy in times of economic distress. Economic groups were clearly incapable of resisting the urge to pursue self-interest in government. The Mugwump concept of an impartial public interest failed to gain much support.

The utilitarian moral standard—the golden rule—may have been above the reach of economic groups, but excessive expectations are no grounds for ridicule. If none believed in moral values or the public interest,

12. McPherson, *Abolitionist Legacy,* 328–29; McFarland, *Mugwumps, Morals, and Politics,* 139–41; Henry Adams, to be sure, might be called a vindictive elitist after he dropped out of Mugwumpery and morality.

then politicians could have continued their spoils system of government hiring and their patriotic wars for foreign glory and flag-waving reelections. Manufacturers could have continued to purchase their special tariff protection, corrupting the Congress. But because Mugwumps lived by standards of public morality, they created a public-interest pressure group that occasionally persuaded politicians to rise above support of private interests.

The old satire of Mugwumps as "carping," "pedantic," "sniveling," despicable elitists, which can be found in John G. Sproat's *"The Best Men"* (1968) should be shelved as a verbal excess of the cultural revolution of the 1960s.[13] The professor would have been nearer the truth if he had suggested that Mugwumps actually shared a kinship with 1960s radicalism. The crusade against the Vietnam war, discrimination, and injustice exhibited a moral passion not unlike that which had produced Mugwumpery. Yes, change occurs in the numbers on the calendar, in the specific remedies for public troubles, and in the styles of protest, but moral concern for the general welfare persists, obsessing the Gilded Age Mugwump and the 1960s New Left. The struggle for meaning, justice, and public morality has been a recurring theme among young Americans. Aging radicals from the Movement culture might recognize their great-great-grandparents among the Mugwumps and embrace rather than reject them.

For 1960s professors to have turned Ben Butler and Henry Cabot Lodge into models of good Americans while making Mugwumps into villains was an indefensible reversal of moral values. The commitments of politicians and moralists are different, but politicians do better work when they are hectored by public moralists who put character and values above self-interest. Mugwumps certainly did not "prostitute" the liberal creed to suit the needs of big business. Any manufacturer or defense contractor could have exposed this canard. The true charge against Mugwumps is that they were Victorian moralists more committed to values than the American majority. They, and not the believing American expansionists, upheld the golden rule in the imperialist debate. They were Christian liberals and not Darwinian liberals. They understood the big issues—money, tariff, civil service, and imperialism—as moral problems requiring citizens to defend life, liberty, and property of individuals rather than the demands of special interests. They were moralists but not prudes. They thought Grover Cleveland's private sins less damaging to the general welfare than James

---

13. Sproat, *"The Best Men,"* 271, 273–81.

G. Blaine's public sins. They were moralists but not Evangelicals; they advocated human freedom but not school bible reading or prohibition of beer and wine.

Perhaps the Mugwump sense of republican virtue had become archaic. And yet, is it nostalgia to think the citizen is obligated to support the "public interest" over and against private interests? These public moralists still look good in their time and place. They should never be written off as only frustrated conservatives. Mugwumps were activists for individual rights of life, liberty, and property. They made war on the corrupting influence of partisanship. Even if we do not share their confidence in the free market and limited government, they still speak to our democracy in their insistence that politicians and citizens need instruction from public moralists if they are to rise above personal and private interests.

Bibliography

Manuscript Collections

Mugwump correspondence has generally been published. Important unpublished collections are:

Adams Family Papers. Massachusetts Historical Society. Available on microfilm.
Edward Atkinson Papers. Massachusetts Historical Society.
David A. Wells Papers. Library of Congress. Available on microfilm.

Books and Articles

Adams, Charles Francis, Jr. *An Autobiography.* Boston: Houghton Mifflin, 1916.
Adams, Henry. *The Education of Henry Adams.* Boston: Massachusetts Historical Society, 1918.
Armstrong, William M. *E. L. Godkin: A Biography.* Albany: State University of New York Press, 1978.
————. *E. L. Godkin and American Foreign Policy.* New York: Bookman, 1957.
————. "The Freedmen's Movement and the Founding of the *Nation.*" *Journal of American History* 53 (March 1967): 708–26.
Armstrong, William M., ed. *The Gilded Age Letters of E. L. Godkin.* Albany: State University of New York Press, 1974.
Barclay, Thomas S. "The Liberal Republican Movement in Missouri." *Missouri Historical Quarterly* 20–21 (October 1925–October 1926).
Beisner, Robert L. *Twelve against Empire: The Anti-imperialists.* New York: McGraw-Hill, 1968.

Blau, Joseph L. *Men and Movements in American Philosophy.* Englewood Cliffs: Prentice-Hall, 1952.

Blodgett, Geoffrey. *The Gentle Reformers: Massachusetts Democrats in the Cleveland Era.* Cambridge: Harvard University Press, 1966.

——. "The Mugwump Reputation, 1870 to the Present." *Journal of American History* 66 (March 1980): 867–87.

Butler, Benjamin F. *Butler's Book.* Boston: Thayer, 1892.

Chalfant, Edward. *Better in Darkness: A Biography of Henry Adams, His Second Life, 1862–1891.* Hamden: Archon Books, 1994.

——. *Both Sides of the Ocean: A Biography of Henry Adams, His First Life, 1838–1862.* Hamden: Archon Books, 1982.

Clark, Clifford E. "Religious Beliefs and Social Reforms in the Gilded Age: The Case of Henry Whitney Bellows." *New England Quarterly* 43 (March 1970): 59–78.

Collini, Stefan. *Public Moralists: Political Thought and Intellectual Life in Britain, 1850–1930.* Oxford: Oxford University Press, 1991.

Dawson, William Harbutt. *Richard Cobden and Foreign Policy.* London: George Allen and Unwin, 1926.

Downey, Matthew T. "Horace Greeley and the Politicians: The Liberal Republican Convention in 1872." *Journal of American History* 53 (March 1967): 727–50.

Ferleger, Herbert Ronald. *David A. Wells and the American Revenue System, 1865–1870.* New York: H. R. Ferleger, 1942.

Fleming, E. McClung. *R. R. Bowker: Militant Liberal.* Norman: University of Oklahoma Press, 1952.

Fuess, Claude Moore. *Carl Schurz: Reformer.* New York: Dodd, Mead, 1932.

Garraty, John A. *Henry Cabot Lodge: A Biography.* New York: Alfred A. Knopf, 1953.

Gerber, Richard Allan. "The Liberal Republicans of 1872 in Historiographical Perspective." *Journal of American History* 62 (June 1975): 40–73.

Grimes, Alan Pendleton. *The Political Liberalism of the New York Nation, 1865–1932.* Chapel Hill: University of North Carolina Press, 1953.

Godwin, Parke. *A Biography of William Cullen Bryant.* 2 vols. New York: D. Appleton, 1883.

Harmond, Richard. "The 'Beast' in Boston: Benjamin F. Butler as Governor of Massachusetts." *Journal of American History* 55 (September 1968): 266–80.

Harrington, Fred H. "The Anti-imperialist Movement in the United States,

1898–1900." *Mississippi Valley Historical Review* 22 (September 1935): 211–30.

Haskell, Daniel C. *The Nation Index, 1865–1917.* New York: New York Public Library, 1951.

Haskell, Thomas L. "Capitalism and the Origins of Humanitarian Sensibility." *American Historical Review* 90 (April and June 1985): 339–61, 547–66.

———. *The Emergence of Professional Social Science.* Urbana: University of Illinois Press, 1977.

Himmelfarb, Gertrude. *On Liberty and Liberalism: The Case of John Stuart Mill.* New York: Alfred Knopf, 1974.

Hinde, Wendy. *Richard Cobden: A Victorian Outsider.* New Haven: Yale University Press, 1987.

Hixon, William B., Jr. *Moorfield Storey and the Abolitionist Tradition.* New York: Oxford University Press, 1972.

Hofstadter, Richard. *The Age of Reform.* New York: Alfred Knopf, 1955.

Hoogenboom, Ari. *Outlawing the Spoils: A History of the Civil Service Reform Movement.* Urbana: University of Illinois Press, 1961.

Horowitz, Daniel. "Genteel Observers: New England Economic Writers and Industrialization." *New England Quarterly* 48 (March 1975): 65–83.

Howe, Daniel Walker. *The Unitarian Conscience: Harvard Moral Philosophy, 1805–1861.* Cambridge: Harvard University Press, 1970.

Howe, M. A. DeWolfe. *Portrait of an Independent: Moorfield Storey.* Boston: Houghton Mifflin, 1932.

Ions, Edmund. *James Bryce and American Democracy, 1870–1922.* New York: Humanities Press, 1970.

Joyner, Fred Bunyan. *David Ames Wells: Champion of Free Trade.* Cedar Rapids: Torch Press, 1939.

Kirkland, Edward Chase. *Charles Francis Adams Jr.* Cambridge: Harvard University Press, 1965.

Kloppenberg, James T. "The Virtues of Liberalism: Christianity, Republicanism, and Ethics in Early American Political Discourse." *Journal of American History* 74 (June 1987): 9–33.

Krug, Mark M. *Lyman Trumbull: Conservative Radical.* New York: A. S. Barnes, 1965.

Lafeber, Walter. *The New Empire: An Interpretation of American Expansion, 1860–1898.* Ithaca: Cornell University Press, 1963.

Levenson, J. C., Ernest Samuels, Charles Vandersee, and Viola Hopkins

Winner, eds. *The Letters of Henry Adams.* 6 vols. Cambridge: Harvard University Press, 1982–1988.

Livingston, James. *Origins of the Federal Reserve System: Money, Class, and Corporate Capitalism.* Ithaca: Cornell University Press, 1986.

Logsdon, Joseph. *Horace White: Nineteenth Century Liberal.* Westport: Greenwood, 1971.

Lowell, James Russell. *Literary and Political Addresses.* Boston: Houghton Mifflin, 1890.

Mann, Arthur. *Yankee Reformers in the Urban Age.* Cambridge: Harvard University Press, 1954.

McFarland, Gerald W. *Mugwumps, Morals, and Politics, 1884–1920.* Amherst: University of Massachusetts Press, 1975.

McGerr, Michael E. *The Decline of Popular Politics: The American North, 1865–1928.* New York: Oxford University Press, 1986.

McJimsey, George T. *Genteel Partisan: Manton Marble.* Ames: Iowa State University Press, 1971.

McKivigan, John R. *The War against Proslavery Religion: Abolitionism and the Northern Churches.* Ithaca: Cornell University Press, 1984.

Meyer, D. H. *The Instructed Conscience: The Shaping of the American National Ethic.* Philadelphia: University of Pennsylvania Press, 1972.

Mill, John Stuart. *Autobiography.* New York: Columbia, 1924.

———. *Principles of Political Economy.* Abridged by J. Laurence Laughlin. New York: D. Appleton, 1884.

Milne, Gordon. *George William Curtis and the Genteel Tradition.* Bloomington: Indiana University Press, 1956.

Morgan, H. Wayne. *From Hayes to McKinley: National Party Politics.* Syracuse: Syracuse University Press, 1969.

Morison, Elting E., John Blum, and John J. Buckley, eds. *The Letters of Theodore Roosevelt.* Vol. 1. Cambridge: Harvard University Press, 1951.

Morris, Edmund. *The Rise of Theodore Roosevelt.* New York: Coward, McCann and Geoghegan, 1979.

Murray, James O. *Francis Wayland.* Boston: Houghton Mifflin, 1891.

Nevins, Allan, and Milton Halsey Thomas, eds. *The Diary of George Templeton Strong.* 4 vols. New York: Macmillan, 1952.

Norton, Charles Eliot. *Considerations on Some Recent Social Theories.* Boston: Little, Brown, 1853.

Norton, Charles Eliot, ed. *Orations and Addresses of George William Curtis.* 2 vols. New York: Harper, 1893.

Norton, Sara, and M. A. DeWolfe Howe, eds. *Letters of Charles Eliot Norton.* 2 vols. Boston: Houghton Mifflin, 1913.

Ogden, Rollo, ed. *Life and Letters of Edwin Lawrence Godkin.* 2 vols. New York: Macmillan, 1907.

Osborne, Thomas J. *"Empire Can Wait": American Opposition to Hawaiian Annexation.* Kent: Kent State University Press, 1981.

Packe, Michael St. John. *The Life of John Stuart Mill.* New York: Macmillan, 1954.

Parrish, William E. *Missouri under Radical Rule.* Columbia: University of Missouri Press, 1965.

Peterson, Norma L. *Freedom and Franchise: The Political Career of B. Gratz Brown.* Columbia: University of Missouri Press, 1965.

Putnam, George Haven. *Memories of a Publisher, 1865–1915.* New York: G. P. Putnam's, 1915.

Reitano, Joanne. *The Tariff Question in the Gilded Age.* University Park: Pennsylvania State University Press, 1994.

Robson, J. M., ed. *Collected Works of John Stuart Mill.* 21 vols. Toronto: University of Toronto Press, 1965–1969.

Rodgers, Daniel T. "Republicanism: The Career of a Concept." *Journal of American History* 79 (June 1992): 11–38.

Ross, Earle Dudley. *The Liberal Republican Movement.* New York: Henry Holt, 1919.

Samuels, Ernest. *The Young Henry Adams.* Cambridge: Harvard University Press, 1948.

———. *Henry Adams: The Major Phase.* Cambridge: Harvard University Press, 1964.

Sawrey, Robert D. *Dubious Victory: The Reconstruction Debate in Ohio.* Lexington: University Press of Kentucky, 1992.

Schmidt, George P. *The Old Time College President.* Columbia University Studies in the Social Sciences, no. 317. New York: Columbia University Press, 1930.

Schurz, Carl. *The Reminiscences of Carl Schurz.* Vol. 2. New York: Doubleday, Page, 1907.

Sharkey, Robert P. *Money, Class, and Party: An Economic Study of Civil War and Reconstruction.* Baltimore: Johns Hopkins Press, 1959.

Simpson, Brooks D. *The Political Education of Henry Adams.* Columbia: University of South Carolina Press, 1996.

Smith, Wilson. *Professors and Public Ethics: Studies of Northern Moral*

Philosophers before the Civil War. Ithaca: Cornell University Press, 1956.

Socolofsky, Homer E., and Allan B. Spetter. *The Presidency of Benjamin Harrison.* Lawrence: University Press of Kansas, 1987.

Solomon, Barbara M. *Ancestors and Immigrants: A Changing New England Tradition.* Cambridge: Harvard University Press, 1956.

Sproat, John G. *"The Best Men": Liberal Reformers in the Gilded Age.* New York: Oxford University Press, 1968.

Stevenson, Elizabeth. *Park Maker: A Life of Frederick Law Olmsted.* New York: Macmillan, 1977.

Summers, Mark Wahlgren. *The Era of Good Stealings.* New York: Oxford University Press, 1993.

Taussig, Frank William. *The Tariff History of the United States.* New York: G. P. Putnam's, 1888.

Terrill, Tom E. "David A. Wells, the Democracy, and Tariff Reduction, 1877–1894." *Journal of American History* 56 (December 1969): 540–55.

———. *The Tariff, Politics, and American Foreign Policy, 1874–1901.* Westport: Greenwood, 1973.

Thelen, David P. "Rutherford B. Hayes and the Reform Tradition in the Gilded Age." *American Quarterly* 22 (Summer 1970): 150–65.

Thompson, Margaret Susan. *The "Spider Web": Congress and Lobbying in the Age of Grant.* Ithaca: Cornell University Press, 1985.

Timberlake, Richard H., Jr. *The Origins of Central Banking in the United States.* Cambridge: Harvard University Press, 1978.

Tompkins, E. Berkeley. *Anti-imperialism in the United States: The Great Debate, 1890–1920.* Philadelphia: University of Pennsylvania Press, 1970.

Tomsich, John. *A Genteel Endeavor: American Culture and Politics in the Gilded Age.* Stanford: Stanford University Press, 1971.

Trefousse, Hans L. *Carl Schurz: A Biography.* Knoxville: University of Tennessee Press, 1982.

Turner, James. *Without God, Without Creed: The Origins of Unbelief in America.* Baltimore: Johns Hopkins University Press, 1985.

Unger, Irwin. *The Greenback Era.* Princeton: Princeton University Press, 1964.

Vanderbilt, Kermit. *Charles Eliot Norton: Apostle of Culture in a Democracy.* Cambridge: Harvard University Press, 1959.

Van Deusen, Glyndon G. *Horace Greeley: Nineteenth-Century Crusader.* Philadelphia: University of Pennsylvania Press, 1953.

Van Riper, Paul P. *History of the United States Civil Service*. Evanston: Row, Peterson, 1958.

Veysey, Laurence R. *The Emergence of the American University*. Chicago: University of Chicago Press, 1965.

Wall, Joseph Frazier. *Henry Watterson: Reconstructed Rebel*. New York: Oxford University Press, 1956.

Wayland, Francis. *The Elements of Moral Science*. 1835. Reprint, ed. Joseph L. Blau, Cambridge: Harvard University Press, Belknap Press, 1963.

————. *The Elements of Political Economy*. New York: Leavitt, Lord, 1837.

————. *Thoughts on the Present Collegiate System in the United States*. Boston: Gould, Kendall & Lincoln, 1842.

Wayland, Francis, Jr., and H. L. Wayland. *A Memoir of the Life and Labors of Francis Wayland*. New York: Sheldon, 1867.

Weinstein, Allen. *Prelude to Populism: Origins of the Silver Issue, 1867–1878*. New Haven: Yale University Press, 1970.

Welch, Richard E., Jr. *The Presidencies of Grover Cleveland*. Lawrence: University Press of Kansas, 1988.

————. *Response to Imperialism: The United States and the Philippine-American War*. Chapel Hill: University of North Carolina Press, 1979.

Williamson, Harold Francis. *Edward Atkinson: The Biography of an American Liberal*. Boston: Old Corner Bookstore, 1934.

Index

Adams, Brooks, 75, 100
Adams, Charles Francis, Jr.: and loss of faith, 10, 12; and new party, 52, 75, 78; covers currency debate, 61–63; and panic of 1893, 100; supports McKinley, 105
Adams, Charles Francis, Sr.: moral tradition, 7; and paper money, 19; model for sons, 42; and republican virtue, 50–51; reluctant candidate in 1872, 51–53; and Christian republican virtue, 73, 74; candidate in 1876, 76
Adams, Henry: at Harvard, 7, 8; and greenback inflation, 22–23; and new party, 35, 46, 56, 75, 77; and expiration of moral law, 38; and civil service reform, 41, 42; marries, 58; *Democracy*, 71, 76–77; and republican virtue, 74–75; leaves activism to youngsters, 77; stockholder in *Evening Post*, 78; identifies real issues, 81; rejects liberalism, 100–101, 124
Adams, Henry Carter, 89
Adams, John, 73
Adams, John Quincy, II, 51
Adams family values, 7, 42
African Americans: and Mugwumps, 48–49, 113, 114, 124
Allison, William Boyd, 63
Altruism. *See* Benevolence
American Commonwealth, 86
American Economic Association, 95
Anti-Imperialist League, 115–18
Armstrong, William M., 10
Atkinson, Edward: and E. L. Godkin, 13, 30–31; and free market, 24, 120; and free

trade, 27, 30, 31, 88; and new party, 35, 54, 56, 57; and currency expansion, 63, 105; anti-imperialist, 113, 117; defends Mugwumps, 119; forced from tariff reform, 121; mentioned, 18

Banking reform: sponsored by Mugwumps, 99, 102–3. *See also* Federal Reserve Act
Benevolence: and Mugwumps, viii, ix, 121–22; and markets, 4, 120; and John Stuart Mill, 11–12; secular, 21; and Edward Atkinson, 121–22
Bimetallism, 67
Blaine, James G., 36, 76, 79
Bland, Richard P., 68
Bland-Allison Act, 68, 69, 70
Bloody-shirt politics, 47–49, 84
Boston Daily Advertiser: and 1884 election, 83
Boutwell, George, 41, 42, 116
Bowen, Francis, 7, 22, 27, 66–67
Bowker, R. R., 77–78, 88
Bowles, Samuel, 46, 54, 55, 57, 75
Bradford, Gamaliel, 115
Bristow, Benjamin H., 75
Brown, Gratz, 50, 55
Bryan, William Jennings, 104, 117, 118
Bryant, William Cullen, 16, 46, 56
Brycè, James, 86
Bullion Report, 64
Bundy, Hezekiah, 62
Butler, Benjamin F.: no Mugwump, viii, 20, 39, 42

Cameron, Don, 100
Cameron, Elizabeth, 100

Hoar, George F., 119
Hofstadter, Richard, vii, 22, 39
Hoogenboom, Ari, vii, 39, 41, 42
Hooper, Marian, 58, 100

Immigrants: and corruption, 42;
Mugwump view of, 123
Imperialism: and young Republicans,
109–11
Inflation: and quantity theory of money,
17; and salaried classes, 17–18; and
Mugwump interests, 18–19; erodes
virtue, 21–25; and social mobility,
22–24; violation of natural rights,
24–25; and silver, 95–106
Interstate Commerce Commission, 120
Irish analogy, 48–49

James, Edmund J., 95
Jenckes, Thomas A., 40, 44
Jones, John Percival, 66

Kelley, William D., 31, 62

Labor unions: and Mugwumps, 123
Laughlin, J. Laurence, 104
Liberalism: classical, 4–5; secular, 10–14;
and money, 15, 24–25, 62–67; and
tariff, 26–27; and Liberal Republican
party, 55–58; anniversary of *Wealth
of Nations*, 59; and Mugwump revolt,
82–84, 86–88; and Democratic party,
90–94; criticized by new school, 95–96;
abandoned by Henry Adams, 100–101;
defended by Mugwumps, 101–6; and
anti-imperialism, 107–18; and banking
reform, 120
Liberal Republicans: origins of, 46; issues,
50, 57
Lodge, Henry Cabot: advised by Henry
Adams, 74; new party, 75; leaves reform,
80; defends tariff, 93, 100; imperialist,
109, 110; anti-immigrant, 123
Lowell, James Russell, 123

Mahan, Alfred Thayer, 109
Market economy: and moral philosophy,
4–5; not characterized by corruption,
24; and Cobden Club, 33; and money,
95; and Mugwumps, 120–21
Massachusetts Reform Club, 80
McCulloch, Hugh, 17, 31, 35

McFarland, Gerald W., 81
McKim, James, 13
McKinley, William: too unprincipled, 103;
becomes lesser evil, 103–4; elected, 105;
imperialism, 111, 114, 118
McKinley Tariff, 93, 97
Mill, John Stuart: and moral philosophy,
10–11; priest of liberals, 11–12; and U.S.
Civil War, 12; trust, 24; tariff, 27, 37;
civil service, 40, 45; mentioned, 62, 83,
88, 101, 107, 108
Million, 83
Mills, Roger Q., 91–92
Missouri reform, 46–47
Monetary Commission, 66
Money. *See* Greenbacks; Silver; Inflation
Moral collapse, 20–24, 38, 42, 73–74
Morality: taught in moral philosophy,
1–3; in free market, 4; and slavery,
5–7; and John Stuart Mill, 11–12; and
Mugwumps, 13–14, 125–26; and money
question, 15–16, 18–19, 23–25; and
status resentment, 22–25, 39–42; and
tariff, 26. *See also* Christian ethics;
Virtue; Moral philosophy
Moral philosophy: key for Mugwump
behavior, viii, ix, 7; required college
course, 1–5; and slavery, 5–7; at Harvard,
7–8; and Charles Eliot Norton, 8; and
E. L. Godkin, 10; and John Stuart Mill,
11–12; and Mugwumps, 14; and money,
15–16, 19; and Mugwump revolt,
124–26
Morton, Oliver P., 61, 62
Mugwumps: negative interpretations of,
vii, 22, 39, 119, 125; characteristics of,
vii-x, 119–26; secular moralists, 13–14,
74–75; pessimism of, 59–60, 71–72,
76–77; origin of name, 73; and bolt of
1884, 79–85; liberalism of, 83–84; and
W. J. Bryan, 104–5; and banking reform,
105–6, 120; and war, 107–8; Cobdenites,
110, 116–17; not Social Darwinists, 112,
113, 125; benevolence of, 121–22

Nation: liberalism, 9–10, 13–14; and
Atkinson, 13, 30–31; and free trade,
13–14, 46; inflation, 71; refinanced,
78–79; and Cleveland, 85, 91; tariff, 93;
and Ely, 102, and McKinley election, 103
Newcomb, Simon, 65
New economists, 89, 95–96